D1135608

bread

100 everyday recipes

First published in 2012
LOVE FOOD is an imprint of Parragon Books Ltd

Parragon
Chartist House
15-17 Trim Street
Bath BA1 1HA, UK

www.parragon.com/lovefood

ISBN: 978-1-4454-9871-3

Printed in China

Produced by Ivy Contract
Cover and new internal photography by Clive Bozzard-Hill
Cover and new home economy by Christine France

Notes for the Reader

This book uses both metric and imperial measurements. Follow the same units of measurement throughout; do not mix metric and imperial. All spoon measurements are level: teaspoons are assumed to be 5 ml, and tablespoons are assumed to be 15 ml. Unless otherwise stated, milk is assumed to be full fat, eggs and individual vegetables are medium, and pepper is freshly ground black pepper. Unless otherwise stated, all root vegetables should be washed in plain water and peeled prior to using. Garnishes, decorations and serving suggestions are all optional and not necessarily included in the recipe ingredients or method.

The times given are an approximate guide only. Preparation times differ according to the techniques used by different people and the cooking times may also vary from those given. Optional ingredients, variations or serving suggestions have not been included in the time calculations.

Recipes using raw or very lightly cooked eggs should be avoided by infants, the elderly, pregnant women, convalescents and anyone suffering from an illness. Pregnant and breastfeeding women are advised to avoid eating peanuts and peanut products. Sufferers from nut allergies should be aware that some of the ready-made ingredients used in the recipes in this book may contain nuts. Always check the packaging before use. The publisher has been careful to select ingredients for the recipes used in the gluten-free chapter that will not cause a problem for anyone who is sensitive to gluten. However, always read labels carefully and, if necessary, check with the manufacturer.

bread

introduction

There is little to beat the satisfaction of making your own bread, when you create something scrumptiou from a bowlful of unpromising ingredients. Kneading dough is a fabulous stress-buster, and making you own bread is a genuinely pleasurable activity with the bonus of delicious edible results. Baking bread is very sociable experience – family and friends will crowd into the kitchen, drawn by the enticing aroma c the thought of bringing traditional favourites to life. And there is something truly wonderful about the wa freshly baked bread smells, the crunch of the crust, and its warm, soft texture.

Bread is cheap to make, and a lot simpler than you might think. The basic skills of bread-makin are very easy to learn, and you need little in the way of specialist equipment beyond a sieve, woode spoon, large mixing bowl, loaf tins, baking sheets and a wire rack. And although several hours may elaps between starting and finishing the process, for quite a lot of that time you can do other things.

These 100 recipes feature an enticing selection of breads, from the humble white loaf to multi-seeded concoctions and exotic variations from all over the world. There are also chapters on savoury and sweet breads and, finally, a selection of gluten-free breads that are sure to become firm favourites. Just add some chopped nuts, seeds, dried fruit or grated cheese and the recipes listed here can multiply into endless mouthwatering variations. The sheer variety of styles and flavours you can use when making bread means you can easily create something delightful for every taste.

With a little practice, a novice bread-maker can quickly gain confidence and be inspired to bake delicious and unusual breads. The results will enchant friends and family alike. From recipes for wholesome wholemeal loaves to flatbreads, focaccias and french baguettes, you will find plenty of inspiration on the following pages to create great bread for any occasion.

basic breads & rolls

crusty white bread

ingredients

makes 1 loaf

1 egg
1 egg yolk
150–200 ml/5–7 fl oz
    lukewarm water
500 g/1 lb 2 oz strong white flour,
    plus extra for dusting
1½ tsp salt
2 tsp sugar
1 tsp easy-blend dried yeast
25 g/1 oz butter, diced
sunflower oil, for brushing

method

1 Place the egg and egg yolk in a jug and beat lightly to mix. Add enough lukewarm water to make up to 300 ml/10 fl oz. Stir well.

2 Sift the flour into a bowl and stir in the salt, sugar and yeast. Add the butter and rub it in with your fingertips until the mixture resembles breadcrumbs. Make a well in the centre, add the egg mixture and work to a smooth dough.

3 Turn out onto a lightly floured surface and knead well for about 10 minutes, or until smooth. Brush a bowl with oil. Place the dough in the bowl and cover with a damp tea towel. Leave to rise in a warm place for 1 hour, or until doubled in size.

4 Brush a 900-g/2-lb loaf tin with oil. Turn out the dough onto a lightly floured surface and knead for 1 minute, or until smooth. Shape the dough the length of the tin and 3 times the width. Fold the dough in 3 lengthways and place it in the tin with the join underneath. Cover with a tea towel and leave in a warm place for 30 minutes, or until it has risen above the tin. Meanwhile, preheat the oven to 220°C/425°F/Gas Mark 7. Place in the preheated oven and bake for 30 minutes, or until firm and golden brown. Transfer to a wire rack to cool.

wholemeal harvest bread

ingredients

makes 1 loaf

225 g/8 oz strong wholemeal flour,
plus extra for dusting

1 tbsp skimmed milk powder

1 tsp salt

2 tbsp soft light brown sugar

1 tsp easy-blend dried yeast

1½ tbsp sunflower oil,
plus extra for brushing

175 ml/6 fl oz lukewarm water

method

1 Put the flour, milk powder, salt, sugar and yeast into a bowl. Make a well in the centre, pour in the oil and add the water, then mix well to make a smooth dough.

2 Turn out onto a lightly floured surface and knead well for about 10 minutes, or until smooth. Brush a bowl with oil. Shape the dough into a ball, place it in the bowl and cover with a damp tea towel. Leave to rise in a warm place for 1 hour, or until doubled in size.

3 Brush a 900-g/2-lb loaf tin with oil. Turn out the dough onto a lightly floured surface and knead for 1 minute, or until smooth. Shape the dough the length of the tin and 3 times the width. Fold the dough into 3 lengthways and place it in the tin with the join underneath. Cover and leave in a warm place for 30 minutes, or until it has risen above the tin. Meanwhile, preheat the oven to 220°C/425°F/Gas Mark 7.

4 Place the bread in the preheated oven and bake for 30 minutes, or until firm and golden brown. Transfer to a wire rack to cool.

granary bread

ingredients

makes 1 loaf

500 g/1lb 2 oz granary bread flour,
plus extra for dusting
1 tbsp olive oil, plus extra for
brushing
1½ tsp salt
1 sachet easy-blend dried yeast
1 tbsp clear honey
250 ml/9 fl oz warm water

method

1 Put the flour into a bowl and stir in the oil, salt and yeast. Make a well in the centre, add the honey to the water, pour into the flour mixture and mix to form a soft dough. If it is very sticky add a little more flour.

2 Turn the dough out onto a lightly floured surface and knead for 10 minutes.

3 Return the dough to the mixing bowl and cover with lightly oiled clingfilm. Leave in a warm place for about 1½ hours, or until doubled in size.

4 Turn the dough out and knead again gently for 1 minute. Brush a 900-g/2-lb loaf tin with oil. Put the dough in the tin, cover and leave in a warm place to rise again for about 30 minutes. Meanwhile, preheat the oven to 200°C/400°F/Gas Mark 6.

5 Bake the loaf for 35–40 minutes, or until firm and golden brown. Transfer to a wire rack to cool.

quick grant loaf

ingredients

makes 1 loaf

15 g/½ oz fresh yeast
1 tsp caster sugar
400 ml/14 fl oz lukewarm water
500 g/1 lb 2 oz strong
    wholemeal flour
1 tsp salt
oil, for brushing

method

1 Stir the yeast and sugar into 100 ml/3½ fl oz of the water, then leave to stand for about 10 minutes, or until frothy.

2 Put the flour into a bowl and stir in the salt. Make a well in the centre and add the yeast mixture and remaining water, mixing thoroughly to a very soft dough.

3 Brush a 900-g/2-lb loaf tin with oil. Transfer the dough into the prepared tin and place the tin in a large polythene bag. Leave to rise in a warm place for about 1 hour, or until the dough reaches the top of the tin. Meanwhile, preheat the oven to 200°C/400°F/Gas Mark 6.

4 Bake the loaf in the preheated oven for 30–35 minutes, or until firm and golden brown. Transfer to a wire rack to cool.

half & half loaf

ingredients

makes 1 loaf

350 g/12 oz strong white flour,
    plus extra for dusting
175 g/6 oz strong wholemeal flour
1 sachet easy-blend dried yeast
1½ tsp salt
350 ml/12 fl oz lukewarm water
2 tbsp olive oil
vegetable oil, for brushing

method

1 Sift 250 g/9 oz of the white flour into a bowl, and mix
   the remainder with the wholemeal flour in a separate
   bowl. Add half the yeast and half the salt to each bowl.

2 Make a well in the centre of each flour mix and add
   about half the water and oil to each bowl, mixing to
   a soft dough. The two mixtures should be about the
   same consistency.

3 Turn out the doughs onto a lightly floured surface
   and knead separately for 10 minutes, or until smooth.
   Return the doughs to the separate mixing bowls. Cove
   and leave to rest for 5 minutes.

4 Brush a 900-g/2-lb loaf tin with oil. Turn out the
   doughs, shape each into a smooth round and place
   one round in each end of the prepared tin. Cover and
   leave in a warm place for about 1 hour, or until risen
   just above the top of the tin. Meanwhile, preheat the
   oven to 230°C/450°F/Gas Mark 8.

5 Bake the loaf in the preheated oven for 5 minutes, then
   reduce the oven temperature to 200°C/400°F/Gas Mark 6
   and bake for a further 25–30 minutes, or until firm and
   golden brown. Transfer to a wire rack to cool.

mixed seed bread

ingredients

makes 1 loaf

375 g/13 oz strong white flour,
    plus extra for dusting
125 g/4½ oz rye flour
1½ tsp salt
1½ tbsp skimmed milk powder
1 tbsp soft light brown sugar
1 tsp easy-blend dried yeast
1½ tbsp sunflower oil,
    plus extra for brushing
2 tsp lemon juice
300 ml/10 fl oz lukewarm water
1 tsp caraway seeds
½ tsp poppy seeds
½ tsp sesame seeds

topping

1 egg white
1 tbsp water
1 tbsp sunflower seeds or
    pumpkin seeds

method

1 Put the flours into a bowl and stir in the salt, milk powder, sugar and yeast. Pour in the oil and add the lemon juice and water. Stir in the seeds and mix well to make a smooth dough. Turn out onto a lightly floured surface and knead well for about 10 minutes, or until smooth and elastic.

2 Brush a bowl with oil. Shape the dough into a ball, place it in the bowl and cover with a damp tea towel. Leave to rise in a warm place for 1 hour, or until doubled in size.

3 Brush a 900-g/2-lb loaf tin with oil. Turn out the dough onto a lightly floured surface and knead for 1 minute, or until smooth. Shape the dough the length of the tin and 3 times the width. Fold the dough in 3 lengthways and place it in the tin with the join underneath. Cover with a tea towel and leave in a warm place for 30 minutes, or until it has risen above the tin. Meanwhile, preheat the oven to 220°C/425°F/Gas Mark 7.

4 For the topping, lightly beat the egg white with the water to make a glaze. Brush the glaze over the loaf, then gently press the sunflower seeds all over the top.

5 Bake in the preheated oven for 30 minutes, or until firm and golden brown. Transfer to a wire rack to cool.

seven-grain bread

ingredients

makes 1 loaf

40 g/1½ oz wholegrain millet
300 g/10½ oz strong
    wholemeal flour
200 g/7 oz plain white spelt flour,
    plus extra for dusting
1 sachet easy-blend dried yeast
1½ tsp salt
40 g/1½ oz rye flakes
40 g/1½ oz rolled oats
40 g/1½ oz polenta,
    plus extra for sprinkling
2 tbsp sesame seeds
350 ml/12 fl oz lukewarm water
1 tbsp olive oil
1 tbsp white wine vinegar
vegetable oil, for brushing

method

1 Bring a saucepan of water to the boil, add the millet, bring back to the boil and simmer for 10 minutes. Drain well.

2 Combine the wholemeal flour and spelt flour in a bowl and stir in the yeast and salt. Stir in the rye flakes, oats, polenta, cooked millet and sesame seeds and mix well. Make a well in the centre and add the water, oil and vinegar, mixing to a soft dough.

3 Turn out the dough onto a lightly floured surface and knead for about 10 minutes. Place the dough back in the mixing bowl, cover and leave to rest for 5 minutes.

4 Brush a baking sheet with oil. Turn out the dough and knead lightly until smooth, then shape into a large round loaf. Sprinkle the prepared baking sheet with polenta, place the dough on the sheet and slash the top with a sharp knife in a criss-cross pattern.

5 Cover and leave in a warm place for about 1 hour, or until doubled in size. Meanwhile, preheat the oven to 220°C/425°F/Gas Mark 7.

6 Bake in the preheated oven for 10 minutes, then reduce the oven temperature to 200°C/400°F/Gas Mark 6 and bake for a further 20–25 minutes, or until firm and golden brown. Transfer to a wire rack to cool.

sunflower twist

ingredients

makes 1 loaf

300 g/10½ oz strong white flour,
    plus extra for dusting
200 g/7 oz strong wholemeal flour
1 sachet easy-blend dried yeast
1½ tsp salt
250 ml/9 fl oz lukewarm water
100 ml/3½ fl oz apple juice
1 tbsp sunflower oil,
    plus extra for brushing
100 g/3½ oz sunflower seeds
milk, for glazing

method

1 Sift the white flour into a bowl, add the wholemeal
flour and stir in the yeast and salt. Make a well in the
centre and add the water, apple juice and oil, mixing to
a soft dough.

2 Turn out the dough onto a lightly floured surface and
knead for about 10 minutes. Place the dough back in
the mixing bowl, cover and leave to rest for 5 minutes.

3 Brush a baking sheet with oil. Turn out the dough and
knead in about two thirds of the sunflower seeds.
Divide the dough in half and shape each piece into a
25-cm/10-inch long sausage shape. Twist the 2 pieces
of dough together, firmly pinching the ends to seal.

4 Place on the prepared baking sheet, leaving room for
spreading. Cover and leave in a warm place for about
1 hour, or until doubled in size. Meanwhile, preheat the
oven to 230°C/450°F/Gas Mark 8.

5 Brush the dough with milk and sprinkle with the
remaining sunflower seeds. Bake in the preheated oven
for 10 minutes, then reduce the oven temperature to
220°C/425°F/Gas Mark 7 and bake for a further 20–25
minutes, or until firm and golden brown. Transfer to a
wire rack to cool.

plaited poppy seed bread

ingredients

makes 1 loaf

225 g/8 oz strong white flour, plus
    extra for dusting
1 tsp salt
2 tbsp skimmed milk powder
1¼ tbsp sugar
1 tsp easy-blend dried yeast
175 ml/6 fl oz lukewarm water
2 tbsp sunflower oil,
    plus extra for brushing
5 tbsp poppy seeds

topping

1 egg yolk
1 tbsp milk
1 tbsp caster sugar
2 tbsp poppy seeds

method

1 Sift the flour and salt together into a bowl, and stir in the milk powder, sugar and yeast. Pour in the water and oil and mix to a soft dough.

2 Turn out the dough onto a lightly floured surface and knead for 1–2 minutes. Add the poppy seeds.

3 Divide the dough into 3 equal pieces and shape each piece into a rope about 25–30 cm/10–12 inches long. Place the ropes side by side and pinch them together at one end. Plait the dough, and pinch the other end together, tucking it underneath.

4 Brush a baking sheet with oil. Place the plait on the prepared baking sheet, cover with lightly oiled clingfilm and set aside in a warm place for about 30 minutes to rise. Preheat the oven to 200°C/400°F/Gas Mark 6.

5 To make the topping, lightly beat the egg yolk with the milk and caster sugar to combine. Remove the clingfilm from the plait, brush the top with the egg glaze and sprinkle over poppy seeds. Bake in the preheated oven for 30–35 minutes, or until firm and golden brown. Transfer to a wire rack to cool.

corn bread

ingredients
makes 1 loaf

vegetable oil, for brushing
175 g/6 oz plain flour
1 tsp salt
4 tsp baking powder
1 tsp caster sugar
280 g/10 oz polenta
115 g/4 oz butter, softened
4 eggs
250 ml/9 fl oz milk
3 tbsp double cream

method

1 Preheat the oven to 200°C/400°F/Gas Mark 6. Brush a 20-cm/8-inch square cake tin with oil.

2 Sift the flour, salt and baking powder together into a bowl. Add the sugar and polenta and stir to mix. Add the butter and cut it into the dry ingredients with a knife, then rub in with your fingertips until the mixture resembles breadcrumbs.

3 Lightly beat the eggs in a bowl with the milk and cream, then stir into the polenta mixture until thoroughly combined.

4 Spoon the mixture into the prepared tin and smooth the surface with a palette knife. Bake in the preheated oven for 30–35 minutes, or until a skewer inserted into the centre of the loaf comes out clean. Remove the tin from the oven and leave to cool for 5–10 minutes, then cut into squares and serve warm.

rye bread

ingredients

makes 1 loaf

225 g/8 oz strong white flour,
    plus extra for dusting
450 g/1 lb rye flour
2 tsp salt
2 tsp soft light brown sugar
1 sachet easy-blend dried yeast
425 ml/15 fl oz lukewarm water
2 tsp vegetable oil,
    plus extra for brushing
1 egg white

method

1 Sift the white flour into a bowl, add the rye flour and
   stir in the salt, sugar and yeast. Make a well in the
   centre and pour in the water and oil. Stir until the
   dough begins to come together, then knead until it
   leaves the side of the bowl. Turn out onto a lightly
   floured surface and knead for 10 minutes, or until
   elastic and smooth. Shape the dough into a ball, put
   into a bowl brushed with oil, cover and leave to rise in
   warm place for 2 hours, or until doubled in size.

2 Brush a baking sheet with oil. Turn out the dough onto
   a lightly floured surface and knead for 10 minutes.
   Shape the dough into a ball, put it on the prepared
   baking sheet and cover. Leave to rise in a warm place
   for a further 40 minutes, or until doubled in size.

3 Meanwhile, preheat the oven to 190°C/375°F/Gas Mark 5
   Beat the egg white with 1 tablespoon of water in a
   bowl. Bake the loaf in the preheated oven for
   20 minutes, then remove from the oven and brush the
   top with the egg white glaze. Return to the oven and
   bake for a further 20 minutes.

4 Remove from the oven, brush the top of the loaf with
   the glaze again and return to the oven for a further
   20–30 minutes, or until the crust is a rich brown colour
   Transfer to a wire rack to cool.

pumpernickel bread

ingredients

makes 1 loaf

200 g/7 oz strong white flour,
    plus extra for dusting
250 g/9 oz rye flour
1 sachet easy-blend dried yeast
1½ tsp salt
2 tsp caraway seeds
1 tbsp black treacle
300 ml/10 fl oz lukewarm water
oil, for brushing
beaten egg, for glazing

method

1 Sift the white flour into a bowl, add the rye flour, stir in the yeast, salt and caraway seeds, then make a well in the centre. Dissolve the black treacle in the water and stir into the dry ingredients, mixing to a soft dough.

2 Turn out the dough onto a lightly floured surface and knead for about 10 minutes. Return the dough to the mixing bowl, cover and leave to rest for 5 minutes.

3 Brush a baking sheet with oil. Turn out the dough and knead briefly for 1 minute. Shape into an oval about 35 cm/14 inches long. Place on the prepared baking sheet and slash the top diagonally at intervals with a sharp knife.

4 Cover and leave in a warm place for about 1 hour, or until doubled in size. Meanwhile, preheat the oven to 190°C/375°F/Gas Mark 5.

5 Bake the loaf in the preheated oven for 20 minutes. Mix the egg with 1 tablespoon of cold water and brush over the loaf to glaze. Reduce the oven temperature to 180°C/350°F/Gas Mark 5, return the loaf to the oven and bake for a further 20–25 minutes, or until firm. Transfer to a wire rack to cool.

sourdough bread

ingredients

makes 2 loaves

450 g/1 lb wholemeal flour
4 tsp salt
350 ml/12 fl oz lukewarm water
2 tbsp black treacle
1 tbsp vegetable oil,
    plus extra for brushing
plain flour, for dusting

starter

85 g/3 oz wholemeal flour
85 g/3 oz strong white flour
55 g/2 oz caster sugar
250 ml/9 fl oz milk

method

1 First, make the starter. Put the flours, sugar and milk into a non-metallic bowl and beat well with a fork. Cover with a damp tea towel and leave to stand for 4–5 days, or until it is frothy and smells sour.

2 Put the flour and half the salt into a bowl and add the water, treacle, vegetable oil and sourdough starter. Mix well with a wooden spoon until a dough begins to form, then knead with your hands until it leaves the side of the bowl. Turn out on to a lightly floured surface and knead for 10 minutes, or until smooth and elastic.

3 Form the dough into a ball and put it into a bowl brushed with oil. Cover and leave to rise in a warm place for 2 hours, or until doubled in size. Dust 2 baking sheets with flour. Mix the remaining salt with 4 tablespoons of water in a bowl. Turn out the dough on to a lightly floured surface and knead for a further 10 minutes. Halve the dough, shape each piece into an oval and place on the prepared baking sheets. Brush with the salt water glaze and leave to stand in a warm place, brushing frequently with the glaze, for 30 minutes. Preheat the oven to 220°C/425°F/Gas Mark 7.

4 Brush the loaves with the remaining glaze and bake for 30 minutes, or until firm and golden brown. Transfer to wire racks to cool.

saffron finger rolls

ingredients
makes 12

1 tsp saffron strands
3 tbsp boiling water
500 g/1 lb 2 oz strong white flour,
    plus extra for dusting
1 sachet easy-blend dried yeast
1½ tsp salt
300 ml/10 fl oz lukewarm milk
2 tbsp melted butter,
    cooled slightly
vegetable oil, for brushing

method

1 Place the saffron in a small bowl and pour over the boiling water. Leave to stand for 30 minutes.

2 Sift the flour into a bowl and stir in the yeast and salt. Make a well in the centre and add the milk, butter and saffron with its liquid, mixing to a soft dough.

3 Turn out the dough onto a lightly floured surface and knead for about 10 minutes until smooth. Place the dough back in the mixing bowl, cover and leave to rest for 5 minutes.

4 Brush a large baking sheet with oil. Turn out the dough and lightly knead, then divide into 12 pieces and shape each into a 10-cm/4-inch long finger shape.

5 Place the rolls on the prepared baking sheet about 2.5cm/1 inch apart and use a sharp knife to cut a shallow lengthways slash on top of each. Cover and leave in a warm place for about 1 hour, or until the rolls are doubled in size and almost touching. Meanwhile, preheat the oven to 220°C/425°F/Gas Mark 7.

6 Bake the rolls in the preheated oven for 15–20 minutes or until golden brown. Transfer to a wire rack to cool.

hamburger buns

ingredients

makes 8

450 g/1 lb strong white flour, plus
    extra for dusting
1½ tsp salt
2 tsp caster sugar
1 tsp easy-blend dried yeast
150 ml/5 fl oz lukewarm water
150 ml/5 fl oz lukewarm milk
vegetable oil, for brushing
2–3 tbsp sesame seeds

method

1 Sift the flour and salt together into a bowl and stir in
the sugar and yeast. Make a well in the centre and pou
in the water and milk. Stir well until the dough begins
to come together, then knead until it leaves the side c
the bowl. Turn out onto a lightly floured surface and
knead for about 10 minutes, or until smooth and elast

2 Brush a bowl with oil. Shape the dough into a ball, pu
it in the bowl and cover. Leave to rise in a warm place
for 1 hour, or until doubled in size.

3 Brush 2 baking sheets with oil. Turn out the dough
onto a lightly floured surface and knead briefly. Divide
it into 8 equal pieces, shape each into a ball and put
them on the prepared baking sheets. Flatten slightly
with a lightly floured hand and cover. Leave to rise in
warm place for 30 minutes. Meanwhile, preheat the
oven to 200°C/400°F/Gas Mark 6.

4 Lightly press the centre of each bun with your fingers
to release any large air bubbles. Brush the tops with
the oil and sprinkle with sesame seeds. Bake for
15–20 minutes, or until light golden brown. Transfer
to a wire rack to cool.

crusty white rolls

ingredients

makes 12

125 ml/4 fl oz milk
4 tbsp water
5 tbsp butter, softened,
    plus extra for greasing
350 g/12 oz strong white flour,
    plus extra for dusting
½ tsp salt
1½ tsp easy-blend dried yeast
1 tbsp sugar
1 extra large egg, beaten
sunflower oil, for brushing

method

1 Put the milk, water, and half of the butter into a saucepan and heat gently until combined. Sift the flour and salt together into a bowl and stir in the yeast and sugar. Make a well in the centre and slowly pour in half of the milk mixture, then mix in the egg. Slowly stir in the remaining milk mixture until a soft dough forms.

2 Brush a bowl with oil. Turn out the dough onto a lightly floured surface and knead for 8–10 minutes, or until smooth and elastic. Put the dough into the bowl, cover and set aside for 1 hour, or until doubled in size.

3 Turn out the dough onto a lightly floured surface and knead for 1–2 minutes. Cover and leave for 10 minutes. Preheat the oven to 200°C/400°F/Gas Mark 6 and dust a baking sheet with flour. Melt the remaining butter in a small saucepan over medium heat.

4 Roll out the dough to a thickness of 5 mm/¼ inch. Stamp out 12 rounds with an 8-cm/¼-inch rounds cutter. Brush the middle of each rounds with butter, fold over and pinch the edges together to seal. Place on the prepared baking sheet.

5 Lightly brush the tops of the rolls with butter and bake in the preheated oven for 12–15 minutes, or until firm and golden brown. Transfer to a wire rack to cool.

cashew nut rolls

ingredients

makes 8

85 g/3 oz cashew nuts
500 g/1 lb 2 oz strong white flour,
    plus extra for dusting
1 sachet easy-blend dried yeast
1½ tsp salt
250 ml/9 fl oz lukewarm water
100 ml/3½ fl oz lukewarm milk
vegetable oil, for brushing
beaten egg, for glazing

method

1 Roughly chop 2 tablespoons of the nuts and grind the remainder in a food processor, or finely chop.

2 Sift the flour into a bowl and stir in the yeast, salt and ground nuts. Make a well in the centre and add the water and milk, mixing to a soft dough.

3 Turn out the dough onto a lightly floured surface and knead for about 10 minutes until smooth. Place the dough back in the mixing bowl, cover and leave to rest for 5 minutes.

4 Brush a baking sheet with oil. Turn out the dough and lightly knead, then divide into 8 pieces and shape each piece into a 25-cm/10-inch long sausage shape. Loosely tie each length of dough into a knot and place on the prepared baking sheet, leaving room for spreading.

5 Cover and leave in a warm place for about 1 hour, or until doubled in size. Meanwhile, preheat the oven to 220°C/425°F/Gas Mark 7.

6 Brush the rolls with the beaten egg and sprinkle with the chopped nuts. Bake in the preheated oven for 15–20 minutes, or until firm and golden brown. Transfer to a wire rack to cool.

english muffins

ingredients

makes 8

500 g/1 lb 2 oz strong white flour,
    plus extra for dusting
1 sachet easy-blend dried yeast
1 tsp salt
1 tsp sugar
200 ml/7 fl oz lukewarm water
150 g/5½ oz natural yogurt
semolina, for sprinkling
sunflower oil, for brushing

method

1 Sift the flour into a bowl and stir in the yeast, salt and sugar. Make a well in the centre and add the water and yogurt, mixing to a soft dough.

2 Turn out the dough onto a lightly floured surface and knead for 10 minutes, or until smooth. Place the dough back in the mixing bowl, cover and leave to rest for 5 minutes.

3 Turn out the dough and roll out to a thickness of about 2 cm/¾ inch. Stamp out 8 rounds with a 7.5-cm/3-inch round cutter.

4 Sprinkle a baking sheet with semolina, arrange the muffins on top and sprinkle with semolina. Cover and leave in a warm place for about 1 hour, or until doubled in size.

5 Heat a griddle pan or heavy-based frying pan until very hot and brush with oil. Add the muffins and reduce the heat to medium, then cook in batches for about 12 minutes, turning once, or until firm and golden brown. Transfer to a wire rack to cool.

bagels

ingredients

makes 10

350 g/12 oz strong white flour,
    plus extra for dusting
2 tsp salt
1 sachet easy-blend dried yeast
1 tbsp lightly beaten egg
200 ml/7 fl oz lukewarm water
vegetable oil, for brushing

glaze

1 egg white
2 tsp water
2 tbsp caraway seeds

method

1 Sift the flour and salt together into a bowl and stir in the yeast. Make a well in the centre, pour in the egg and the water and mix to a dough. Turn out onto a lightly floured surface and knead well for about 10 minutes, or until smooth. Brush a bowl with oil. Shape the dough into a ball, place it in the bowl and cover. Leave to rise for 1 hour, or until doubled in size.

2 Brush 2 baking sheets with oil and dust a sheet with flour. Turn out the dough onto a lightly floured surface and knead for 2 minutes. Divide into 10 pieces, shape each into a ball and leave to rest for 5 minutes. Flatten each ball with a lightly floured hand and make a hole in the centre. Put the bagels on the floured sheet, cover and leave to rise for 20 minutes.

3 Meanwhile, preheat the oven to 220°C/425°F/Gas Mark 7 and bring a saucepan of water to the boil. Reduce the heat until the water is barely simmering, then add 2 bagels. Poach for 1–2 minutes, turning over in the water. Remove with a slotted spoon and drain on a tea towel. Poach the remaining bagels in the same way. Transfer the bagels to the prepared baking sheets. Beat the egg white with the water in a bowl and brush it over the bagels. Sprinkle with the caraway seeds and bake in the preheated oven for 25–30 minutes, or until golden brown. Transfer to a wire rack to cool.

breadsticks

ingredients

makes 30

350 g/12 oz strong white flour,
    plus extra for dusting
1½ tsp salt
1 sachet easy-blend dried yeast
200 ml/7 fl oz lukewarm water
3 tbsp olive oil, plus extra
    for brushing
sesame seeds, for coating

method

1 Sift the flour and salt together into a bowl. Stir in the
   yeast. Make a well in the centre. Add the water and oil
   to the well and mix to form a soft dough.

2 Turn out the dough onto a lightly floured work surface
   and knead for 5–10 minutes, or until smooth and
   elastic. Put the dough in an oiled bowl, cover and leave
   to rise for 1 hour, or until doubled in size.

3 Preheat the oven to 200°C/400°F/Gas Mark 6. Brush 2
   baking sheets with oil.

4 Turn out the dough again and knead lightly. Roll out
   into a rectangle measuring 23 x 20 cm/9 x 8 inches. Cut
   the dough into 3 strips, each 20 cm/8 inches long, then
   cut each strip across into 10 equal pieces.

5 Roll and stretch each piece of dough into a stick about
   30 cm/12 inches long, then brush with oil. Spread out
   the sesame seeds on a large shallow plate or sheet. Roll
   each breadstick in the sesame seeds to coat, then
   space well apart on the prepared baking sheets. Brush
   with oil, cover and leave to rise for 15 minutes.

6 Bake in the preheated oven for 10 minutes. Turn over
   and bake for a further 5–10 minutes, or until golden.
   Transfer to a wire rack and leave to cool.

savoury breads

sun-dried tomato rolls

ingredients

makes 8

225 g/8 oz strong white flour,
   plus extra for dusting
½ tsp salt
1 sachet easy-blend dried yeast
100 g/3½ oz butter, melted and
   cooled slightly, plus extra for
   greasing
3 tbsp milk, warmed
2 eggs, beaten
50 g/1¾ oz sun-dried tomatoes,
   drained and finely chopped
milk, for brushing

method

1 Sift the flour and salt together into a bowl. Stir in the
   yeast, then pour in the butter, milk and eggs. Mix
   together to form a dough.

2 Turn the dough onto a lightly floured work surface and
   knead for about 5 minutes.

3 Brush a bowl with butter. Place the dough in the bowl,
   cover and leave to rise for 1–1½ hours, or until
   doubled in size.

4 Meanwhile, preheat the oven to 230°C/450°F/Gas Mark 8.
   Lightly grease a baking sheet. Turn out the dough and
   knead for approximately 2–3 minutes. Knead the
   sun-dried tomatoes into the dough, sprinkling the
   work surface with extra flour as the tomatoes are
   quite oily.

5 Divide the dough into 8 balls and place them on the
   prepared baking sheet. Cover and leave to rise for about
   30 minutes, or until the rolls have doubled in size.

6 Brush the rolls with milk and bake in the preheated
   oven for 10–15 minutes, or until golden brown. Transfer
   to a wire rack to cool.

cherry tomato, rosemary & sea salt focaccia

ingredients

makes 1 loaf

5 tbsp olive oil, plus extra for brushing

2 garlic cloves, crushed

350 g/12 oz strong white flour, plus extra for dusting

2 tsp salt

1 sachet easy-blend dried yeast

1 tsp caster sugar

225 ml/8 fl oz lukewarm water

2 tsp finely chopped fresh rosemary

200–225g/7–8 oz ripe red cherry tomatoes

1/4 tsp flaky sea salt

method

1 Mix together 2 tablespoons of the oil and all of the garlic. Set aside. Sift the flour and salt together in a bowl and stir in the yeast and sugar. Add the remaining oil and water. Mix to a dough. Turn out onto a lightly floured surface and knead for 10 minutes until smooth and elastic, then knead in 1 tablespoon of the garlic-flavoured oil.

2 Brush a 17 x 25-cm/6½ x 10-inch baking tin with oil. Press the dough over the base of the tin with your hands. Brush with the remaining garlic oil, then scatter over the rosemary. Cover loosely with clingfilm and set aside in a warm place for about 1 hour until puffed up and doubled in size.

3 Preheat the oven to 230°C/450°F/Gas Mark 8. Scatter the tomatoes over the focaccia and press them into the base of the dough. Sprinkle with the sea salt. Place in the preheated oven and immediately reduce the temperature to 200°C/400°F/Gas Mark 6. Bake for 25–30 minutes, or until firm and golden brown. Transfer to a wire rack to cool.

bruschetta with tomato, red onion & basil salsa

ingredients

serves 6

1 large baguette (see page 106)
2 tbsp basil oil

salsa

2 red onions
10 g/¼oz fresh basil leaves
10 plum tomatoes, peeled,
    deseeded and diced
juice of 2 lemons
salt and pepper

method

1 Preheat the oven to 230°C/450°F/Gas Mark 8.

2 Slice open the baguette and place on a baking sheet. Brush with some of the oil and place in the oven. Toas until golden brown.

3 Chop the onions and basil and combine with the tomatoes, lemon juice and the remaining oil. Add salt and pepper to taste. Spoon the salsa over each slice o toasted bread and serve.

wholemeal carrot rolls

ingredients

makes 8

250 g/9 oz strong white flour,
    plus extra for dusting
250 g/9 oz strong wholemeal flour,
    plus extra for sprinkling
1 sachet easy-blend dried yeast
1½ tsp salt
300 ml/10 fl oz lukewarm water
2 tbsp olive oil
175 g/6 oz carrots, finely grated
vegetable oil, for brushing

method

1 Sift the white flour into a bowl, add the wholemeal flour and stir in the yeast and salt. Make a well in the centre and add the water, olive oil and carrots, mixing to a soft dough.

2 Turn out the dough onto a lightly floured surface and knead for about 10 minutes until smooth. Place the dough in a bowl, cover and leave to rest for 5 minutes.

3 Brush a baking sheet with oil. Turn out the dough and lightly knead again until smooth. Divide into 8 pieces, shape each piece into a ball and arrange on the prepared baking sheet, leaving room for spreading.

4 Cover and leave in a warm place for about 1 hour, or until doubled in size. Meanwhile, preheat the oven to 220°C/425°F/Gas Mark 7.

5 Sprinkle the rolls with a little wholemeal flour and bake in the preheated oven for 12–15 minutes, or until golden brown. Transfer to a wire rack to cool.

courgette & parmesan bread

ingredients
makes 1 loaf

225 g/8 oz self-raising white flour,
   plus extra for dusting
225 g/8 oz self-raising
   wholemeal flour
1 tsp salt
1½ tsp mustard powder
55 g/2 oz butter, diced,
   plus extra for greasing
225 g/8 oz courgettes, coarsely
   grated and patted dry
140 g/5 oz Parmesan cheese,
   finely grated
1 tsp finely chopped fresh thyme
2 eggs, beaten
about 175 ml/6 fl oz
   semi-skimmed milk
pepper

method

1 Preheat the oven to 190°C/375°F/Gas Mark 5. Grease a baking sheet and set aside. Put the flours into a bowl, stir in the salt, pepper and mustard powder, then lightly rub in the butter until the mixture resembles breadcrumbs. Stir in the courgettes, Parmesan cheese and chopped thyme. Stir in the eggs and enough milk to form a soft dough.

2 Turn the dough onto a lightly floured surface and knead lightly, then shape into a 20-cm/8-inch round. Place on the prepared baking sheet, then cut 3 fairly deep slashes in the top of the loaf using a sharp knife.

3 Bake in the preheated oven for 40–50 minutes, or until well risen and deep golden brown. Transfer to a wire rack to cool. Serve warm or cold in slices, on its own or spread with butter.

variation

Replace the Parmesan cheese with 115 g/4 oz freshly cooked chopped chestnut mushrooms and substitute 2 tablespoons chopped fresh basil for the thyme.

walnut & seed bread

ingredients

makes 2 large loaves

450 g/1 lb wholemeal flour

450 g/1 lb granary flour

115 g/4 oz strong white flour,
plus extra for dusting

2 tbsp sesame seeds

2 tbsp sunflower seeds

2 tbsp poppy seeds

115 g/4 oz walnuts, chopped

2 tsp salt

2 sachets easy-blend dried yeast

2 tbsp olive oil or walnut oil

700 ml/1¼ pints
lukewarm water

1 tbsp melted butter or oil,
for greasing

method

1 Put the flours, seeds, walnuts, salt and yeast into a bowl and mix together. Make a well in the centre, add the oil and water and stir well to form a soft dough. Turn out the dough onto a lightly floured surface and knead well for 5–7 minutes, or until smooth and elastic.

2 Return the dough to the bowl, cover with a damp tea towel and leave in a warm place for 1–1½ hours to rise, or until doubled in size. Turn out onto a lightly floured surface and knead again for 1 minute.

3 Brush 2 x 900-g/2-lb loaf tins well with melted butter or oil. Divide the dough in 2. Shape 1 piece the length of the tin and 3 times the width. Fold the dough in 3 lengthways and place in 1 of the tins with the join underneath. Repeat with the other piece of dough.

4 Cover and leave to rise again in a warm place for about 30 minutes, or until well risen above the tins. Meanwhile, preheat the oven to 230°C/450°F/Gas Mark 8.

5 Bake the loaves in the centre of the preheated oven for 25–30 minutes. If the loaves are getting too brown, reduce the temperature to 220°C/425°F/Gas Mark 7. Transfer to wire racks to cool.

caramelized onion baguettes

ingredients
makes 3 small baguettes

2 tbsp olive oil
1 large onion, thinly sliced
1 garlic clove, thinly sliced
1 tbsp balsamic vinegar
500 g/1 lb 2 oz strong white flour,
    plus extra for dusting
1 sachet easy-blend dried yeast
2 tsp salt
300 ml/10 fl oz lukewarm water
1 tbsp clear honey
vegetable oil, for brushing

method

1 Heat the olive oil in a small frying pan, add the onion and garlic and fry for 8–10 minutes, stirring constantly or until soft. Stir in the balsamic vinegar, then transfer the mixture to a bowl and leave to cool slightly.

2 Sift the flour into a bowl and stir in the yeast and salt. Make a well in the centre and add the water and honey. Stir in the onion mixture and knead to a soft, sticky dough.

3 Turn out the dough onto a lightly floured surface and knead for about 10 minutes, or until evenly mixed and elastic. Cover and leave to rest for 5 minutes.

4 Brush a baking sheet with oil. Divide the dough into 3 pieces, shape each piece into a ball, then roll with your hands to form 30-cm/12-inch long baguette shapes. Place the baguettes on the prepared baking sheet. Slash the tops of the baguettes 4–5 times with a sharp knife. Cover and leave in a warm place for about 1 hour or until doubled in size. Meanwhile, preheat the oven to 230°C/450°F/Gas Mark 8.

5 Spray the preheated oven with water, then place the baguettes in the oven and spray the oven again. Bake for 12–15 minutes, or until golden brown. Transfer to a wire rack to cool.

flatbread with onion & rosemary

ingredients

makes 1 loaf

450 g/1 lb strong white flour, plus
  extra for dusting
½ tsp salt
1 sachet easy-blend dried yeast
2 tbsp chopped fresh rosemary,
  plus small sprigs to garnish
5 tbsp extra virgin olive oil, plus
  extra for brushing
300 ml/10 fl oz lukewarm water
1 red onion, thinly sliced and
  pushed out into rings
1 tbsp coarse sea salt

method

1 Sift the flour and salt together into a bowl and stir in
the yeast and rosemary. Make a well in the centre and
pour in 3 tablespoons of the olive oil and the water. S
well until the dough begins to come together, then
knead until it leaves the side of the bowl. Turn out on
a lightly floured surface and knead well for about
10 minutes, or until smooth and elastic.

2 Brush a bowl with oil. Shape the dough into a ball, pu
in the bowl and cover with a damp tea towel. Leave to
rise in a warm place for 1 hour, or until doubled in size

3 Brush a baking sheet with oil. Turn out the dough on
a lightly floured surface and knead for 1 minute. Roll
out the dough to a round about 30 cm/12 inches in
diameter and put it on the prepared baking sheet.
Cover and leave the dough to rise in a warm place fo
20–30 minutes.

4 Preheat the oven to 200°C/400°F/Gas Mark 6. Using t
handle of a wooden spoon, make indentations all ov
the surface of the loaf. Spread the onion rings over th
top, drizzle with the remaining oil and sprinkle with t
sea salt. Bake for 20 minutes. Sprinkle with the
rosemary sprigs, return to the oven and bake for a
further 5 minutes, or until golden brown. Transfer to
wire rack to cool slightly and serve warm.

garlic bread rolls

ingredients

makes 8

butter, for greasing
12 garlic cloves
350 ml/12 fl oz milk
450 g/1 lb strong white flour
1 tsp salt
1 sachet easy-blend dried yeast
1 tbsp dried mixed herbs
3 tbsp sunflower oil
1 egg, lightly beaten
milk, for brushing
sea salt, for sprinkling

method

1 Grease a baking sheet with a little butter and set aside. Place the garlic cloves and milk in a saucepan, bring to the boil and simmer gently for 15 minutes. Cool slightly then process in a food processor or blender to blend the garlic.

2 Sift the flour and salt together into a bowl, stir in the yeast then add the mixed herbs. Add the garlic-flavoured milk, sunflower oil and beaten egg to the dry ingredients and mix to form a dough.

3 Place the dough on a lightly floured work surface and knead lightly for a few minutes until smooth and soft.

4 Grease a bowl with butter. Place the dough in the bowl, cover and leave to rise in a warm place for about 1 hour, or until doubled in size.

5 Knead the dough for 2 minutes. Divide the dough into 8 pieces and shape into rolls. Score the tops of the rolls with a knife and place them on the prepared baking sheet. Cover and leave to stand for 15 minutes. Preheat the oven to 220°C/425°F/Gas Mark 7.

6 Brush the rolls with milk and sprinkle sea salt over the top. Bake in the preheated oven for 15–20 minutes, or until firm and golden brown. Transfer the rolls to a wire rack to cool.

garlic & sage bread

ingredients

makes 1 loaf

250 g/9 oz strong brown flour, plus
    extra for dusting
1 sachet easy-blend dried yeast
3 tbsp chopped fresh sage
2 tsp sea salt
3 garlic cloves, finely chopped
1 tsp clear honey
150 ml/5 fl oz lukewarm water
vegetable oil, for brushing

method

1 Sift the flour into a bowl and tip in the bran from the
   sieve. Stir in the yeast, sage and half the sea salt.
   Reserve 1 tsp of the garlic and stir the remainder into
   the bowl. Make a well in the centre and pour in the
   honey and water. Stir until the dough begins to come
   together, then knead until it leaves the side of the bo
   Turn out onto a lightly floured surface and knead we
   for about 10 minutes, or until smooth and elastic.

2 Brush a bowl with oil. Shape the dough into a ball, p
   it in the bowl and cover. Leave to rise in a warm plac
   for 1 hour, or until doubled in size.

3 Brush a baking sheet with oil. Turn out the dough on
   a lightly floured surface and knead for 2 minutes. Rol
   the dough into a long sausage, shape into a ring and
   put it onto the prepared baking sheet. Brush the
   outside of a bowl with oil and put it into the centre o
   the ring to prevent it from closing up while the doug
   is rising. Cover with a tea towel and leave to rise in a
   warm place for 30 minutes.

4 Preheat the oven to 200°C/400°F/Gas Mark 6. Remov
   the bowl from the centre of the loaf. Sprinkle the loa
   with the remaining sea salt and the reserved garlic a
   bake for 25–30 minutes, or until firm and golden
   brown. Transfer to a wire rack to cool.

peanut butter bread with onion & thyme

ingredients

makes 1 loaf

500 g/1 lb 2 oz strong white flour,
     plus extra for dusting
1 sachet easy-blend dried yeast
1 tsp salt
300 ml/10 fl oz lukewarm water
1 tbsp olive oil
4 tbsp crunchy peanut butter
1 tsp dried thyme
3 spring onions, finely chopped
vegetable oil, for brushing

method

1 Sift the flour into a bowl and stir in the yeast and salt. Make a well in the centre and stir in the water, oil, peanut butter, thyme and onions, mixing to a soft dough.

2 Turn out the dough onto a lightly floured surface and knead well for about 10 minutes, or until smooth and elastic. Cover and leave to rest for 5 minutes.

3 Brush a baking sheet with oil. Shape the dough into oval and place on the prepared baking sheet. Slash t top of the dough at intervals with a sharp knife. Cove and leave in a warm place for about 1 hour, or until doubled in size. Meanwhile, preheat the oven to 220°C/425°F/Gas Mark 7.

4 Bake the loaf in the preheated oven for 15 minutes, the reduce the oven temperature to 200°C/400°F/Gas Mar and bake for a further 15–20 minutes, or until firm and golden brown. Transfer to a wire rack to cool.

oat & potato bread

ingredients

makes 1 loaf

2 starchy potatoes, cut into chunks
450 g/1 lb strong white flour, plus
    extra for dusting
1 sachet easy-blend dried yeast
1½ tsp salt
1½ tbsp dark brown sugar
3 tbsp rolled oats
2 tbsp skimmed milk powder
40 g/1½ oz slightly salted butter,
    diced
225 ml/8 fl oz lukewarm water
vegetable oil, for brushing

topping

1 tbsp water
1 tbsp rolled oats

method

1 Put the potatoes in a large saucepan, add water to
cover and bring to the boil. Cook for 20–25 minutes, or
until tender. Drain the potatoes, then mash until
smooth. Leave to cool.

2 Sift the flour into a bowl and stir in the yeast, salt, sugar,
oats and milk powder. Rub in the butter with your
fingertips until the mixture resembles breadcrumbs.
Mix in the mashed potatoes, then add the water and
mix to a soft dough.

3 Turn out the dough onto a lightly floured surface and
knead for 5–10 minutes, or until smooth and elastic.
Put the dough in an oiled bowl, cover and leave to rise
in a warm place for 1 hour, or until doubled in size.

4 Brush a 900-g/2-lb loaf tin with oil. Turn out the dough
onto a lightly floured surface and knead lightly. Shape
into a loaf and transfer to the prepared tin. Cover and
leave to rise in a warm place for 30 minutes. Meanwhile,
preheat the oven to 220°C/425°F/Gas Mark 7.

5 Brush the loaf with water and sprinkle over the oats.
Bake in the preheated oven for 25–30 minutes, or until
firm and golden brown. Transfer to a wire rack to cool
slightly. Serve warm.

sub rolls with parsley

ingredients

makes 4

500 g/1 lb 2 oz strong white flour,
  plus extra for dusting
1½ tsp salt
1 sachet easy-blend dried yeast
350 ml/12 fl oz lukewarm water
1 tbsp olive oil
2 tbsp finely chopped fresh parsley
vegetable oil, for brushing

method

1 Sift the flour and salt together into a bowl and stir in the yeast. Make a well in the centre and add the water, olive oil and parsley, mixing to a soft dough.

2 Turn out the dough onto a lightly floured surface and knead for about 10 minutes until smooth. Return the dough to the bowl, cover and leave to rest for 5 minutes.

3 Brush a baking sheet with oil. Turn out the dough and lightly knead, then divide into 4 pieces and shape each piece into a torpedo shape.

4 Place the rolls on the prepared baking sheet, leaving room for spreading. Cover and leave in a warm place for about 1 hour, or until doubled in size. Meanwhile, preheat the oven to 220°C/425°F/Gas Mark 7.

5 Bake the rolls in the preheated oven for 12–15 minutes or until golden brown. Transfer to a wire rack to cool.

tapenade chilli swirls

ingredients

makes 10

500 g/1 lb 2 oz strong white flour,
    plus extra for dusting
1½ tsp sea salt
1 sachet easy-blend dried yeast
350 ml/12 fl oz lukewarm water
2 tbsp olive oil
90 g/3¼ oz ready-made green
    olive tapenade
½ tsp crushed dried chillies
polenta, for sprinkling
2 tbsp finely grated Parmesan
    cheese

method

1 Sift the flour into a bowl and stir in the salt and yeast. Make a well in the centre and add the water and oil, mixing to a soft dough.

2 Turn out the dough onto a lightly floured surface and knead for about 10 minutes, or until smooth. Return the dough to the bowl, cover and leave to rest for 5 minutes.

3 Turn out the dough onto a lightly floured surface and roll out to a 35 x 46-cm/14 x 18-inch rectangle. Spread the tapenade evenly over the dough to within 1 cm/½ inch of the edges. Sprinkle with the chillies.

4 Roll up the dough from one long side to enclose the filling, like a Swiss roll. Sprinkle a large baking sheet with polenta.

5 Using a sharp knife, cut the dough into 10 thick slices and arrange cut side down on the prepared baking sheet. Cover and leave in a warm place for about 1 hour, or until doubled in size. Meanwhile, preheat the oven to 220°C/425°F/Gas Mark 7.

6 Sprinkle the slices with cheese, then bake in the preheated oven for 20–25 minutes, or until well risen and golden brown. Transfer to a wire rack to cool.

olive bread

ingredients

makes 2 medium loaves

900 g/2 lb strong white flour, plus
    extra for dusting

1 tsp salt

1 sachet easy-blend dried yeast

3 tsp sesame seeds

½ tsp dried oregano

3 tbsp olive oil, plus extra
    for brushing

600 ml/1 pint warm water

225 g/8 oz Greek olives,
    stoned and roughly chopped

method

1 Sift the flour and salt together into a large bowl, and s
in the yeast, 2 teaspoons of the sesame seeds and the
oregano. Add the olive oil and gradually add the wate
to form a firm dough.

2 Turn the dough onto a lightly floured work surface an
knead for 10 minutes or until smooth. Put the dough
a clean bowl, cover and leave to rise in a warm place f
about 1 hour or until doubled in size.

3 Brush a baking sheet with oil. Turn the dough onto a
lightly floured work surface and knead lightly to knock
out the air, then knead in the olives. Divide the dough
into 2 and shape each half into a smooth round. Place c
the prepared baking sheet, cover and leave in a warm
place for about 30 minutes, or until doubled in size.
Meanwhile, preheat the oven to 220°C/425°F/Gas Mark

4 Using a sharp knife, make slashes across the top of
each loaf then lightly brush with olive oil and sprinkle
the remaining sesame seeds on top.

5 Bake in the preheated oven for 10 minutes, then
reduce the temperature to 190°C/375°F/Gas Mark 5
and bake for a further 25 minutes, or until firm and
golden brown. Transfer to wire racks to cool.

pesto & olive soda bread

ingredients
makes 1 loaf

350 g/12 oz plain flour
250 g/9 oz wholemeal flour
1 tsp bicarbonate of soda
½ tsp salt
3 tbsp pesto
300 ml/10 fl oz buttermilk
85 g/3 oz stoned green olives,
    roughly chopped
olive oil, for brushing
milk, to glaze

method

1 Preheat the oven to 200°C/400°F/Gas Mark 6. Brush a baking sheet with oil. Sift the flours, bicarbonate of soda and salt together into a bowl, adding back any bran from the sieve.

2 Combine the pesto and buttermilk. Stir into the flour with the olives, mixing to a soft dough. Add more liquid if needed.

3 Shape the dough into a 20-cm/8-inch round and pla on the baking sheet. Flatten slightly and cut a deep cross in the top with a sharp knife.

4 Brush with milk and bake for 30–35 minutes, or until firm and golden brown.

variation

Replace the pesto and olives with 2 tablespoons freshly chopped dill leaves and 2 tablespoons poppy seeds. Ac to the dry ingredients in step 1, reserving a teaspoon of poppy seeds to sprinkle over the top of the loaf in step

olive oil bread with cheese

ingredients

makes 1 loaf

2 sachets dried yeast
1 tsp sugar
250 ml/9 fl oz lukewarm water
350 g/12 oz strong white flour
1 tsp salt
3 tbsp olive oil, plus extra for
    brushing
200 g/7 oz pecorino cheese, cubed
½ tbsp fennel seeds,
    lightly crushed

method

1 Mix the yeast with the sugar and 8 tablespoons of the water. Set aside for about 15 minutes.

2 Sift the flour together with the salt into a bowl. Make a well in the centre. Add 1 tablespoon of the oil, the yeast mixture and the remaining water and mix together to form a smooth dough. Knead the dough for 4 minutes.

3 Brush a baking sheet with oil. Divide the dough into 2 equal portions. Roll out each portion to form a round 5 mm/¼ inch thick. Place 1 round on the prepared baking sheet.

4 Scatter the cheese and half of the fennel seeds evenly over the round. Place the second round of dough on top and squeeze the edges together to seal so that the filling does not leak during the cooking time.

5 Using a sharp knife, make a few slashes in the top of the dough and brush with the remaining oil.

6 Sprinkle with the remaining fennel seeds and set aside to rise for 20–30 minutes. Meanwhile, preheat the oven to 200°C/400°F/Gas Mark 6.

7 Bake in the preheated oven for 30 minutes, or until golden brown. Serve immediately.

cheddar corn bread

ingredients

makes 1 loaf

100 g/3½ oz plain flour
1 tbsp baking powder
pinch of salt
100 g/3½ oz polenta
115 g/4 oz Cheddar cheese, grated
2 eggs, beaten
300 ml/10 fl oz milk
50 g/2 oz butter, melted, plus extra
    for greasing

method

1 Preheat the oven to 200°C/400°F/Gas Mark 6. Grease a
   900-g/2-lb loaf tin with butter and line the base with
   greaseproof paper.

2 Sift the flour, baking powder and salt together into a
   bowl and stir in the polenta and the cheese. Make a
   well in the centre. Add the eggs, milk and butter to the
   well. Gradually incorporate the dry ingredients into the
   liquid until smooth.

3 Pour the mixture into the prepared tin and bake in the
   preheated oven for 40–45 minutes, or until firm and
   golden brown.

4 Leave to cool in the tin for 10 minutes before turning
   out onto a wire rack to cool completely.

spring onion & parmesan polenta bread

ingredients

serves 16

oil, for brushing

140 g/5 oz fine polenta

140 g/5 oz plain flour

4 tsp baking powder

2 tsp celery salt

55 g/2 oz freshly grated
   Parmesan cheese

2 eggs, beaten

400 ml/14 fl oz milk

55 g/2 oz butter, melted

1 bunch spring onions, chopped

pepper

method

1 Preheat the oven to 190°C/375°F/Gas Mark 5. Brush a 23-cm/9-inch square baking tin with oil. Sift the polent flour, baking powder, celery salt and pepper into a bow and stir in 40 g/1½ oz of the Parmesan cheese. Beat together the eggs, milk and melted butter. Add the eg mixture to the dry ingredients and stir well to mix evenly.

2 Stir in the chopped spring onions and spread the mixture evenly into the tin. Sprinkle the remaining Parmesan over the mixture. Bake in the preheated ov for 30–35 minutes, or until firm and golden.

cheese, herb & onion rolls

ingredients

makes 10–12

225 g/8 oz strong white flour
225 g/8 oz granary or malted
　wheat flour
1½ tsp salt
1 tsp mustard powder
1 sachet easy-blend dried yeast
2 tbsp chopped fresh mixed herbs
2 tbsp finely chopped
　spring onions
125–175 g/4½–6 oz Cheddar
　cheese, grated
300 ml/10 fl oz warm water
oil, for brushing
pepper

method

1 Put the flours, salt, mustard and pepper, to taste, into a
　bowl. Stir in the yeast, herbs, spring onions and most of
　the cheese. Add the water to the dry ingredients and m
　to form a firm dough, adding more flour if necessary.

2 Knead until smooth and elastic. Cover and leave in a
　warm place to rise for 1 hour, or until doubled in size.

3 Brush 2 baking sheets with oil. Meanwhile, preheat th
　oven to 200°C/400°F/Gas Mark 6. Knead the dough
　until smooth. Divide into 10–12 pieces and shape into
　round or long rolls, coils or knots. Place on the
　prepared baking sheets, cover and leave to rise until
　doubled in size.

4 Sprinkle with the rest of the cheese. Bake in the
　preheated oven for 15–20 minutes, or until golden
　brown. Transfer to a wire rack to cool.

boxty bread

ingredients

makes 4 small loaves

7 starchy potatoes (about 800 g/
    1 lb 12 oz)
2 tbsp lightly salted butter
150 ml/5 fl oz milk
2 tsp salt
½ tsp black pepper
1½ tsp dill seeds or caraway seeds
    (optional)
400 g/14 oz plain flour,
    plus extra for dusting
5 tsp baking powder

method

1 Preheat the oven to 190°C/375°F/Gas Mark 5. Peel 4 of the potatoes, cut them into even chunks, and bring to boil in a large saucepan of salted water. Cover and simmer gently for about 20 minutes, or until tender. Drain well and put back in the pan. Cover with a clean tea towel for a few minutes to get rid of excess moisture. Mash with the butter until smooth.

2 Meanwhile, peel the remaining 3 potatoes and grate coarsely. Wrap in a clean piece of muslin and squeeze tightly to remove the moisture. Put the grated potato in a large bowl with the milk, ¾ teaspoon of the salt, the pepper and dill seeds, if using. Beat in the mashed potatoes.

3 Sift the flour, baking powder and remaining salt into the potato mixture. Mix to a smooth dough, adding a little more flour if the mixture is too soft.

4 Knead lightly, then shape into 4 flat, round loaves about 10 cm/4 inches in diameter. Place on a nonstick baking sheet. Mark each loaf with a large cross. Bake the preheated oven for 40 minutes, or until well risen and golden brown. Transfer to a wire rack to cool.

cheddar & chive scones

ingredients

makes 12–14

vegetable oil, for brushing
500 g/1 lb 2 oz plain flour
1½ tbsp baking powder
½ tsp salt
½ tsp pepper
125 g/4½ oz butter, diced
150 g/5½ oz mature Cheddar
    cheese, grated
2 tbsp snipped chives
1 large egg
225 ml/8 fl oz buttermilk
    or soured milk

method

1 Preheat the oven to 220°C/425°F/Gas Mark 7. Brush a baking sheet with oil.

2 Sift the flour, baking powder, salt and pepper together into a bowl. Add the butter and rub into the flour with your fingertips until it resembles fine breadcrumbs. Stir in the cheese and chives.

3 Put the egg and buttermilk into a jug and beat together, then stir just enough into the dry ingredients to bind to a soft dough, lightly mixing.

4 Turn out the dough and press together lightly until smooth. Form into a round about 2.5 cm/1 inch thick. Stamp out rounds with a 6-cm/2½-inch cutter and arrange on the prepared baking sheet.

5 Brush with the remaining buttermilk and egg mix. Bake in the preheated oven for 12–15 minutes, or until firm and golden brown. Transfer to a wire rack to cool.

cheese & potato plait

ingredients

makes 1 loaf

175 g/6 oz floury potatoes, diced
2 sachets easy-blend dried yeast
675 g/1 lb 8 oz strong white flour,
    plus extra for dusting
1 tbsp salt
450 ml/16 fl oz vegetable stock
2 garlic cloves, crushed
2 tbsp chopped fresh rosemary
125 g/4½ oz Gruyère cheese,
    grated
1 tbsp vegetable oil,
    plus extra for brushing

method

1 Cook the potatoes in a saucepan of boiling water for 10 minutes, or until soft. Drain and mash the potatoe

2 Transfer the mashed potatoes to a large mixing bowl Stir the yeast, flour, salt and stock into the mashed potatoes and mix together to form a smooth dough. Add the garlic, rosemary and 75 g/2¾ oz of the chee and knead the dough for 5 minutes. Make a hollow ir the dough, pour in the oil and knead the dough.

3 Cover the dough and leave to rise in a warm place fo 1½ hours, or until doubled in size.

4 Brush a baking sheet with oil and lightly dust with flour. Knead the dough again and divide it into 3 equ portions. Roll each portion into a 35-cm/14-inch sausage shape.

5 Pressing 1 end of each of the sausage shapes togeth plait the dough and fold the remaining ends underneath. Place the plait on the baking sheet, cove and leave to rise for 30 minutes. Meanwhile, preheat the oven to 190°C/375°F/Gas Mark 5.

6 Sprinkle the remaining cheese over the top of the pla and bake in the preheated oven for 40 minutes, or ur firm and golden brown. Transfer to a wire rack to coo slightly and serve warm.

cheese & ham loaf

ingredients
makes 1 loaf

225 g/8 oz self-raising flour
1 tsp salt
2 tsp baking powder
1 tsp paprika
85 g/3 oz butter, diced, plus extra
    for greasing
125 g/4½ oz mature Cheddar
    cheese, grated
75 g/2¾ oz smoked ham, chopped
2 eggs, beaten
150 ml/5 fl oz milk

method

1 Preheat the oven to 180°C/350°F/Gas Mark 4. Grease 450-g/1-lb loaf tin with a little butter and line the base with baking paper.

2 Sift the flour, salt, baking powder and paprika into a large mixing bowl.

3 Add the butter and rub it in with your fingertips until the mixture resembles fine breadcrumbs. Stir in the cheese and ham.

4 Add the beaten eggs and milk to the dry ingredients the bowl and mix well. Spoon the cheese and ham mixture into the prepared loaf tin.

5 Bake in the preheated oven for about 1 hour, or until the loaf is well risen and golden brown.

6 Leave the bread to cool in the tin, then turn out and transfer to a wire rack to cool completely. Cut the bread into thick slices to serve.

variation
For a vegetarian option, replace the ham with 1 dessert apple, peeled, cored and cut into small chunks.

breads from around the world

irish stout bread

ingredients

makes 1 loaf

vegetable oil, for brushing
300 ml/10 fl oz stout
250 g/9 oz strong white flour,
    plus extra for dusting
250 g/9 oz malted brown flour
1 sachet easy-blend dried yeast
1½ tsp salt

method

1 Brush a 900-g/2-lb loaf tin with oil. Pour the stout into a saucepan and heat until lukewarm (it should feel neither hot nor cold to the touch). Remove from the heat.

2 Sift the white flour and brown flour into a bowl and s in the yeast and salt. Make a well in the centre and ac the stout, mixing to a soft dough.

3 Turn out the dough onto a lightly floured surface and knead for about 10 minutes until smooth, then retur to the bowl, cover and leave to rest for 5 minutes.

4 Turn out the dough onto a lightly floured surface and lightly knead, then shape into an oval and place in th prepared tin. Cover and leave in a warm place for abo 1 hour, or until doubled in size. Meanwhile, preheat t oven to 230°C/450°F/Gas Mark 8.

5 Place the loaf in the preheated oven, then spray the oven with water. Bake for 10 minutes, then reduce th oven temperature to 200°C/400°F/Gas Mark 6 and ba for a further 20–25 minutes, or until golden brown. Transfer to a wire rack to cool.

irish soda bread

ingredients

makes 1 loaf

butter, for greasing

450 g/1 lb plain flour,
    plus extra for dusting

1 tsp salt

1 tsp bicarbonate of soda

400 ml/14 fl oz buttermilk

method

1 Preheat the oven to 220°C/425°F/Gas Mark 7. Lightly grease a baking sheet.

2 Sift the flour, salt and bicarbonate of soda together in a bowl. Make a well in the centre of the dry ingredients and pour in most of the buttermilk.

3 Mix well together using your hands. The dough should be very soft but not too wet. If necessary, add the remaining buttermilk.

4 Turn out the dough onto a lightly floured surface and knead it lightly. Shape into a 20-cm/8-inch round.

5 Place the bread on the prepared baking sheet, cut a cross in the top and bake in the preheated oven for 25–30 minutes until firm and golden brown. Transfer a wire rack to cool.

variation

To make a fruit soda bread, add 1 tablespoon of caster sugar, the zest of an orange and 115 g/4 oz raisins to the dry ingredients in step 3.

welsh bara brith

ingredients

makes 1 loaf

butter, for greasing
175 ml/6 fl oz milk
4 tsp dried yeast
115 g/4 oz brown sugar
450 g/1 lb strong plain flour
½ tsp salt
115 g/4 oz butter, diced
280 g/10 oz mixed dried fruit
   (sultanas, currants and raisins)
55 g/2 oz mixed peel
1 tsp ground mixed spice
1 egg, beaten

method

1 Grease a 900-g/2-lb loaf tin. Warm the milk in a
saucepan until tepid and add the yeast with 1 teaspoo
of the sugar. Mix well and leave in a warm place for
15 minutes, or until frothy.

2 Sift the flour and salt into a bowl. Rub the butter into
the flour mixture until it resembles breadcrumbs then
add the remaining sugar, dried fruit, peel and mixed
spice and stir well. Add the beaten egg and the frothy
yeast mixture and mix to form a soft dough.

3 Turn the mixture out onto a floured surface and knead
until smooth. Replace the dough in the bowl, cover
and leave in a warm place for 1–1½ hours, or until
doubled in size. Meanwhile, preheat the oven to
190°C/375°F/Gas Mark 5.

4 Turn the dough out again and knead lightly. Shape
the dough into a rectangle the length of the tin and 3
times the width. Fold the dough into 3 lengthways and
put it in the tin with the join underneath. Cover and
leave to rise in a warm place for 30–40 minutes.

5 Bake towards the bottom of the oven for 30 minutes.
Turn the loaf around and cover the top with foil if it is
getting too brown. Continue to cook for a further
30–40 minutes. Transfer to a wire rack to cool.

french baguettes

ingredients

makes 2 loaves

450 g/1 lb strong white flour, plus
extra for dusting
1½ tsp salt
1 sachet easy-blend dried yeast
325 ml/11 fl oz lukewarm water
vegetable oil, for brushing

method

1 Sift the flour and salt into a bowl and stir in the yeast. Make a well in the centre and pour in the water. Stir well until the dough begins to come together, then knead with your hands until it leaves the side of the bowl. Turn out onto a lightly floured surface and knead well for about 10 minutes, or until smooth and elastic.

2 Brush a bowl with oil. Put the dough in the bowl, cover and leave in a warm place for 1 hour, or until doubled in size. Turn out onto a lightly floured surface and knead for 1–2 minutes. Cut the dough in half, shape each piece into a ball and roll out into a rectangle. From 1 long side of a dough rectangle, fold one third over, then fold over the other side. Press gently. Fold the other rectangle in the same way. Cover and leave to rest for 10 minutes. Repeat the rolling and folding twice more, leaving the dough to rest for 10 minutes each time. Gently roll and stretch each piece of dough until it is about 30 cm/12 inches long and an even thickness. Cover and leave to rise for 30–40 minutes.

3 Meanwhile, preheat the oven to 230°C/450°F/Gas Mark 8. Brush 1 or 2 baking sheets with oil. Carefully roll the loaves onto the baking sheets and slash the tops with a sharp knife. Spray the oven with water and bake for 15–20 minutes, or until golden brown. Transfer to a wire rack to cool.

brioche plait

ingredients

makes 1 loaf

350 g/12 oz strong plain white
    flour, plus extra for dusting
½ tsp salt
25 g/1 oz caster sugar
1 sachet easy-blend dried yeast
115 g/4 oz unsalted butter,
    chilled and diced, plus extra
    for greasing
2 eggs, beaten
75 ml/2½ fl oz warm milk
olive oil, for brushing
beaten egg, to glaze

method

1 Sift the flour and salt into a large bowl. Stir in the sugar
  and dried yeast. Add the butter and rub into the flour
  with your fingertips until it resembles breadcrumbs.
  Make a well in the centre and pour the eggs and milk
  into the bowl.

2 Stir well to make a soft dough. Turn the dough onto a
  lightly floured surface and knead for 5–10 minutes until
  smooth and elastic, sprinkling with a little more flour if
  the dough becomes sticky.

3 Brush a large baking sheet with oil. Divide the dough
  into 3 equal pieces and shape each into a rope about
  35 cm/14 inches long. Place the ropes side by side and
  press them together at one end. Plait the ropes then
  pinch the ends together.

4 Transfer the plait to the baking sheet, cover loosely
  with oiled clingfilm and leave in a warm place for
  about 1 hour, or until doubled in size.

5 Preheat the oven to 190°C/375°F/Gas Mark 5. Brush the
  plait with the beaten egg. Bake in the preheated oven
  for 30–35 minutes, or until risen and golden brown,
  covering loosely with foil after 25 minutes to prevent
  over-browning. Serve warm.

salted pretzels

ingredients

makes 16

vegetable oil, for brushing
500 g/1 lb 2 oz strong white flour,
    plus extra for dusting
1 sachet easy-blend dried yeast
1½ tsp salt
1 tbsp dark muscovado sugar
1 tbsp olive oil
350 ml/12 fl oz lukewarm water,
    plus 1 tbsp for brushing
1 tsp bicarbonate of soda
1 egg
coarse sea salt, for sprinkling

method

1 Brush 2 large baking sheets with oil. Sift the flour into bowl and stir in the yeast, salt and sugar. Make a well the centre and stir in the oil with just enough water t mix to a soft dough.

2 Turn out the dough onto a lightly floured surface anc knead for about 10 minutes until smooth. Return to t bowl then cover and leave to rest for 5 minutes.

3 Divide the dough into 16 pieces and roll each piece into a 38-cm/15-inch rope. Lift both ends of the rope and twist together, then drop the ends back over the loop to make pretzel shapes.

4 Place the pretzels on the prepared baking sheets, leaving room for spreading, then cover and leave in a warm place for 20 minutes. Meanwhile, preheat the oven to 220°C/425°F/Gas Mark 7.

5 Bring a large saucepan of water to the boil, add the bicarbonate of soda, then add the pretzels and cook about 20 seconds each, turning once. Remove and drain well, then return to the baking sheets.

6 Beat the egg with the 1 tablespoon of water and bru over the pretzels, then sprinkle with salt. Bake in the preheated oven for 15–20 minutes, or until golden brown. Transfer to a wire rack to cool.

challah

ingredients
makes 1 loaf

vegetable oil, for brushing
500 g/1 lb 2 oz strong white flour,
    plus extra for dusting
1 tsp ground cinnamon
1 sachet easy-blend dried yeast
1 tsp salt
200 ml/7 fl oz lukewarm water
85 g/3 oz clear honey
1 egg, beaten
2 tbsp olive oil

to glaze
1 egg yolk
pinch of salt
1 tbsp water

method

1 Brush a large baking sheet with oil. Sift the flour into
bowl and stir in the cinnamon, yeast and salt. Make a
well in the centre and add the water, honey, egg and
oil, mixing to a soft dough.

2 Turn out the dough onto a lightly floured surface and
knead for about 10 minutes, or until smooth. Return
the bowl then cover and leave in a warm place for
1 hour, or until doubled in size.

3 Turn out the dough onto a lightly floured surface and
lightly knead, then divide into 6 pieces and shape ea
piece into a 35-cm/14-inch long roll. Pinch the ends
the dough together, then plait together, overlapping
from alternate sides. Tuck the end underneath and
place on the prepared baking sheet.

4 Cover and leave in a warm place for about 1 hour, or
until doubled in size. Meanwhile, preheat the oven to
220°C/425°F/Gas Mark 7.

5 Bake in the preheated oven for 15 minutes, then redu
the oven temperature to 190°C/375°F/Gas Mark 5. To
glaze, beat the egg yolk with the salt and water, brush
over the loaf, then return to the oven and bake for a
further 15–20 minutes, or until firm and a rich golden
brown. Transfer to a wire rack to cool.

kulich

ingredients

makes 2 loaves

oil, for brushing
500 g/1 lb 2 oz strong white flour,
    plus extra for dusting
1 sachet easy-blend dried yeast
300 ml/10 fl oz lukewarm milk
1 tsp salt
85 g/3 oz caster sugar
85 g/3 oz butter, melted
    and cooled
2 egg yolks
85 g/3 oz sultanas
40 g/1½ oz flaked almonds
grated rind of 2 oranges
grated rind and juice of 1 lemon
icing sugar and chopped glacé
    fruits, to decorate

method

1 Brush 2 clean terracotta plant pots with a top diameter of 15 cm/6 inches with oil, then line with non-stick baking paper. Place half the flour in a bowl with the yeast and stir in the milk to make a smooth batter. Cover and leave in a warm place for about 20 minutes, or until frothy.

2 Add the remaining flour, salt, sugar, butter, egg yolks, sultanas, almonds, orange rind, lemon rind and 2 tablespoons of the lemon juice and mix to a soft dough. Turn out onto a lightly floured surface and knead for about 10 minutes, or until smooth.

3 Divide the dough into 2 pieces and shape to fit the pots. Cover and leave in a warm place for about 1½ hours, or until risen to the top of the pots. Meanwhile preheat the oven to 220°C/425°F/Gas Mark 7.

4 Bake in the preheated oven for 10 minutes, then reduce the oven temperature to 180°C/350°F/Gas Mark 4 and bake for a further 25–30 minutes, or until firm and golden brown. Turn out and transfer to a wire rack to cool.

5 Mix 2 teaspoons of the lemon juice with enough icing sugar to make a smooth icing, then spoon over the kulich and sprinkle with the glacé fruits.

tuscan unsalted bread

ingredients

*makes 1 large or
2 smaller loaves*

500 g/1 lb 2 oz strong white
    flour, plus extra for dusting
1 sachet easy-blend dried yeast
2 tbsp olive oil, plus extra
    for brushing
300 ml/10 fl oz lukewarm water

method

1 Mix the flour and yeast together in a bowl. Make a we
   in the centre. Mix the olive oil and water together in a
   jug and pour into the well. Gradually mix the liquid in
   the flour mixture with a round-bladed knife. Gather th
   mixture together with your hands to form a soft doug

2 Turn out the dough onto a lightly floured work surfac
   and knead for 5–7 minutes, or until very smooth and
   elastic. Return the dough to the bowl and cover, then
   leave to rise in a warm place for 1 hour, or until doubl
   in size. Turn out and gently knead again for 1 minute,
   until smooth.

3 Preheat the oven to 200°C/400°F/Gas Mark 6. Brush 1
   or 2 baking sheets with oil. Shape the dough into
   1 large oval or 2 smaller ovals and transfer to the
   prepared sheet or sheets. Cover and leave to rise in a
   warm place for 30 minutes.

4 Make several slashes in the top of the bread with a
   sharp knife. Bake in the preheated oven for 30–35
   minutes (or 20–25 minutes for 2 loaves). If the bread
   getting too brown, reduce the temperature a little.
   Transfer to a wire rack to cool.

ciabatta

ingredients

makes 3 loaves

400 ml/14 fl oz lukewarm water
4 tbsp lukewarm
    semi-skimmed milk
500 g/1 lb 2 oz strong white flour
1 sachet easy-blend dried yeast
2 tsp salt
3 tbsp olive oil

biga

350 g/12 oz strong white flour,
    plus extra for dusting
1¼ tsp easy-blend dried yeast
200 ml/7 fl oz lukewarm water

method

1 First, make the biga. Sift the flour into a bowl, stir in the yeast and make a well in the centre. Pour in the water and stir until the dough comes together. Turn out onto a lightly floured surface and knead for 5 minutes, or until smooth and elastic. Put the dough into a bowl, cover and leave to rise in a warm place for 12 hours.

2 Using a wooden spoon, gradually mix the water and milk into the biga. Gradually mix in the flour and yeast with your hand, adding them a little at a time. Finally, mix in the salt and oil. The dough will be very wet; do not add extra flour. Cover and leave to rise in a warm place for 2 hours, or until doubled in size.

3 Dust 3 baking sheets with flour. Using a spatula, divide the dough between the prepared baking sheets without knocking out the air. With lightly floured hands, gently pull and shape each piece of dough into a rectangular loaf, then flatten slightly. Dust the tops of the loaves with flour and leave to rise in a warm place for 30 minutes. Meanwhile, preheat the oven to 220°C/425°F/Gas Mark 7.

4 Bake in the preheated oven for 25–30 minutes, or until the crust is lightly golden. Transfer to wire racks to cool.

herb focaccia

ingredients

makes 1 loaf

400 g/14 oz strong white flour,
    plus extra for dusting
1 sachet easy-blend dried yeast
1½ tsp salt
300 ml/10 fl oz warm water
3 tbsp extra virgin olive oil,
    plus extra for brushing
4 tbsp finely chopped
    fresh mixed herbs
polenta or cornmeal, for sprinkling
sea salt, for sprinkling

method

1 Sift the flour into a bowl and stir in the yeast and salt. Make a well in the centre and gradually stir in the wat and 2 tablespoons of the olive oil to make a dough. Turn the dough out onto a floured work surface and knead for 5 minutes.

2 Transfer to a bowl and lightly knead in the herbs for 10 minutes, or until soft but not sticky. Wash the bowl and lightly brush with olive oil.

3 Place the dough in the oiled bowl, cover and leave in warm place for 1–1½ hours, or until doubled in size. Meanwhile, sprinkle polenta over a baking sheet.

4 Turn the dough out onto a lightly floured surface and knead again for 1–2 minutes. Cover and leave for 10 minutes. Preheat the oven to 230°C/450°F/Gas Mark 8

5 Roll out and pat the dough into a 25-cm/10-inch circle about 1 cm/½ inch thick, and carefully transfer it to th prepared baking sheet. Cover and leave to rise again for 15 minutes. Using a lightly oiled finger, poke indentations all over the surface of the loaf. Drizzle ov the remaining olive oil and sprinkle lightly with sea sa

6 Bake in the preheated oven for 15 minutes, or until golden brown. Transfer to a wire rack to cool.

mini focaccia

ingredients

serves 4

350 g/12 oz strong white flour,
    plus extra for dusting
1 sachet easy-blend dried yeast
½ tsp salt
250 ml/9 fl oz lukewarm water
3 tbsp olive oil, plus extra
    for brushing
100 g/3½ oz stoned green
    or black olives, halved

topping

2 red onions, sliced
2 tbsp olive oil
1 tsp sea salt
1 tbsp thyme leaves

method

1 Sift the flour into a bowl and stir in the yeast and salt. Make a well in the centre and gradually stir in the wa and 2 tablespoons of the olive oil to make a dough. Turn the dough out onto a floured work surface and knead for 5 minutes.

2 Wash the bowl and lightly brush with olive oil. Place the dough in the oiled bowl, cover and leave in a war place for 1–1½ hours, or until doubled in size.

3 Brush a baking sheet with oil. Turn the dough out on a lightly floured surface and knead for 1–2 minutes. Knead half of the olives into the dough, divide the dough into quarters and shape the quarters into circles. Carefully transfer them to the prepared bakin sheet. Using a lightly oiled finger, poke indentations over the surface of the loaves.

4 To make the topping, sprinkle the red onions and remaining olives over the circles. Drizzle the oil over t top and sprinkle with the sea salt and thyme leaves. Cover and leave to stand for 30 minutes. Meanwhile, preheat the oven to 190°C/375°F/Gas Mark 5.

5 Bake in the preheated oven, for 20–25 minutes, or un golden brown. Transfer to a wire rack to cool.

margherita pizza

ingredients

serves 2–4

175 g/6 oz plain flour,
    plus extra for dusting
1 tsp salt
1 tsp easy-blend dried yeast
1 tbsp olive oil, plus extra
    for brushing and drizzling
6 tbsp lukewarm water

topping

175 ml/6 fl oz ready-made pizza
    tomato sauce
1 garlic clove, thinly sliced
55 g/2 oz mozzarella cheese,
    thinly sliced
1 tsp dried oregano
salt and pepper
fresh basil sprigs, to garnish

method

1 Sift the flour and salt together into a bowl and stir in
   the yeast. Make a well in the centre and pour in the oil
   and water. Stir well until the dough begins to come
   together, then knead with your hands until it leaves
   the side of the bowl. Turn out onto a lightly floured
   surface and knead well for 5–10 minutes, or until
   smooth and elastic.

2 Brush a bowl with oil. Shape the dough into a ball, put
   it in the bowl, cover and leave to rise in a warm place
   for 1 hour, or until dough has doubled in size.

3 Brush a baking sheet with oil. Turn out the dough onto
   a lightly floured surface and knead for 1 minute. Roll or
   press out the dough to a 25-cm/10-inch round. Place
   on the prepared baking sheet and push up the edge
   slightly all round. Cover and leave to rise in a warm
   place for 10 minutes. Meanwhile, preheat the oven to
   200°C/400°F/Gas Mark 6.

4 Spread the tomato sauce over the pizza base almost to
   the edge. Sprinkle the garlic over the tomato, add the
   cheese, sprinkle with the oregano and season with salt
   and pepper. Bake the pizza in the preheated oven for
   15–20 minutes, or until the crust is crisp and golden
   brown. Brush the crust with oil, garnish with basil
   sprigs and serve immediately.

calzone

ingredients

serves 4

450 g/1 lb strong white flour,
     plus extra for dusting
1 sachet easy-blend dried yeast
1 tsp salt
300 ml/10 fl oz lukewarm water
1 tbsp olive oil
vegetable oil, for brushing

filling

1 tbsp olive oil
1 red onion, thinly sliced
1 garlic clove, crushed
4 plum tomatoes, chopped
2 tbsp tomato purée
250 g/9 oz cooked ham, diced
2 tbsp chopped fresh basil leaves
200 g/7 oz mozzarella cheese,
     chopped
salt and pepper

method

1 Sift the flour into a bowl and stir in the yeast and salt. Make a well in the centre and add the water and oil, mixing to a soft dough.

2 Turn out the dough onto a lightly floured surface and knead for about 10 minutes until smooth. Return to the bowl, cover and leave in a warm place for 1 hour, or until doubled in size.

3 To make the filling, heat the oil in a frying pan, add the onion and garlic and gently fry for 5 minutes. Add the tomatoes and simmer, stirring, for 5 minutes or until any liquid has evaporated. Remove from the heat and add the tomato purée, ham, basil, and salt and pepper to taste.

4 Preheat the oven to 220°C/425°F/Gas Mark 7 and brush 2 baking sheets with oil. Turn out the dough onto a lightly floured surface and lightly knead. Divide into 4 pieces and shape each piece into a 20-cm/8-inch round.

5 Spoon the filling onto 1 side of each round and top with cheese. Brush the edges with water, fold over to enclose the filling and pinch the edges to seal. Place the prepared baking sheets and pierce a hole in each calzone to let the steam escape. Bake in the preheated oven for 15–20 minutes, or until crisp and golden brown. Serve warm.

grissini with onion seeds

ingredients

makes about 24

300 g/10½ oz strong white flour
150 g/5½ oz strong
     wholemeal flour
1 sachet easy-blend dried yeast
1½ tsp salt
25 g/1 oz black onion seeds
1 tbsp dark muscovado sugar
300 ml/10 fl oz lukewarm water
2 tbsp olive oil, plus extra
     for brushing
coarse sea salt, for sprinkling

method

1 Line 2 large baking sheets with non-stick baking pap

2 Sift the white flour into a bowl, add the wholemeal
  flour and stir in the yeast, salt, onion seeds and sugar
  Make a well in the centre and add the water and oil,
  mixing to a soft dough.

3 Turn out the dough onto a lightly oiled surface and
  lightly knead for about 5 minutes, or until just smoot
  Return to the bowl, cover and leave to stand for abo
  1 hour, or until doubled in size. Meanwhile, preheat t
  oven to 180°C/350°F/Gas Mark 4.

4 Turn out the dough onto a lightly oiled surface and
  lightly knead. Roll out to a 1-cm/½-inch thick square
  Cut into long, pencil-thin strips (a pizza wheel is usef
  here), then arrange down the length of the baking
  sheet, lightly twisting.

5 Brush with oil and sprinkle with salt. Bake in the
  preheated oven for 25–30 minutes, or until golden
  brown and crisp. Carefully transfer to a wire rack to co

pitta breads

ingredients

makes 6–8

350 g/12 oz strong white flour,
    plus extra for dusting
1½ tsp salt
1 tsp caster sugar
1 tsp easy-blend dried yeast
1 tbsp olive oil, plus extra
    for brushing
200 ml/7 fl oz lukewarm water

method

1 Sift the flour and salt together into a bowl and stir in
   the sugar and yeast. Make a well in the centre and pour
   in the oil and water. Stir well until the dough begins to
   come together, then knead with your hands until it
   leaves the side of the bowl. Turn out onto a lightly
   floured surface and knead well for about 10 minutes,
   until smooth and elastic.

2 Shape the dough into a ball, put into an oiled bowl and
   cover. Leave to rise in a warm place for 1 hour, or until
   the dough has doubled in size.

3 Turn out onto a lightly floured surface. Divide the
   dough into 6 to 8 pieces and shape each piece into a
   ball. Cover and leave for 10 minutes.

4 With floured hands, slightly flatten a dough ball and
   roll out on a lightly floured surface to an oval about
   15 cm/6 inches long and 5 mm/¼ inch thick. Place on
   a lightly floured tea towel, sprinkle lightly with flour
   and cover with another tea towel. Repeat with the
   remaining dough balls and leave to rise for 30 minutes.

5 Meanwhile, put 2 or 3 baking sheets in the oven and
   preheat to 230°C/450°F/Gas Mark 8. Transfer the pitta
   breads to the heated baking sheets, spacing them well
   apart, and bake for 5 minutes, or until puffed up and
   golden brown. Transfer to wire racks to cool.

sesame bread rings

ingredients

makes 16

vegetable oil, for brushing

500 g/1 lb 2 oz strong white flour,
    plus extra for dusting

1 sachet easy-blend dried yeast

2 tsp salt

1 tsp ground cumin

1 tsp ground coriander

350 ml/12 fl oz lukewarm water

2 tbsp olive oil

1 egg, beaten

85 g/3 oz sesame seeds

method

1 Brush 2–3 large baking sheets with oil. Sift the flour in a bowl and stir in the yeast, salt, cumin and coriander. Make a well in the centre and add the water and oil, mixing to a soft dough.

2 Turn out the dough onto a lightly floured surface and knead for about 10 minutes, or until smooth. Return the dough to the bowl then cover and leave to rest for 5 minutes.

3 Turn out the dough, divide into 16 pieces and shape each piece into a 35-cm/14-inch rope. Shape into ring pinching the ends together.

4 Beat the egg with 1 tablespoon of cold water and brush over the rings, then dip into the sesame seeds coat and place on the prepared baking sheets. Cover and leave in a warm place for about 1 hour, or until well risen and springy to the touch. Meanwhile, preheat the oven to 220°C/425°F/Gas Mark 7.

5 Bake in the preheated oven for 10–15 minutes, or un firm and golden brown. Transfer to wire racks to cool.

naan bread

ingredients

makes 10

850 g/1 lb 14 oz strong white flour
1 tbsp baking powder
1 tsp sugar
1 tsp salt
350 ml/12 fl oz lukewarm water
1 egg, beaten
4 tbsp melted ghee or vegetable
    oil, plus a little extra for
    greasing and brushing
fresh coriander sprigs, to garnish

method

1 Sift the flour, baking powder, sugar and salt into a bo
   and make a well in the centre. Mix the water and egg
   together, beating until the egg breaks up and is
   blended with the liquid.

2 Slowly add the liquid mixture to the well in the dry
   ingredients, using your fingers to draw in the flour fro
   the side, or until a stiff, heavy dough forms. Shape th
   dough into a ball, cover and leave for 30 minutes.

3 Turn out the dough onto a surface brushed with
   melted ghee and flatten with a rolling pin. Gradually
   sprinkle the dough with the melted ghee and knead
   work it in, little by little. Shape the dough into 10 equ
   balls, cover and leave to rise for 1 hour. Meanwhile,
   preheat the oven to 230°C/450°F/Gas Mark 8 or its
   highest setting.

4 Using a lightly greased rolling pin, roll the dough bal
   into teardrop shapes, about 3 mm/⅛ inch thick. Brus
   2 baking sheets with ghee and arrange the naans on
   the prepared sheets. Bake in the preheated oven for
   5–6 minutes until the naans are golden brown and
   lightly puffed. Serve immediately, garnished with fre
   coriander sprigs.

chilli cornbread

ingredients

serves 8

140 g/5 oz cornmeal
70 g/2½ oz plain flour
1 tbsp baking powder
1 small onion, finely chopped
1–2 fresh green chillies, such as
    jalapeño, deseeded and
    chopped
4 tbsp corn or vegetable oil
125 g/4½ oz canned
    creamed-style sweetcorn
225 ml/8 fl oz sour cream
2 eggs, beaten

method

1 Preheat the oven to 180°C/350°F/Gas Mark 4.

2 Place the cornmeal, flour and baking powder in a large bowl, then stir in the onion and chillies.

3 Heat the oil in a 23-cm/9-inch heavy frying pan with a heatproof handle, tipping the pan to coat the bottom and sides with the oil.

4 Make a well in the centre of the ingredients in the bowl. Add the corn, sour cream, and eggs, then pour in the hot oil from the frying pan. Stir lightly until combined. Pour into the hot frying pan and smooth the surface with a palette knife.

5 Bake in the preheated oven for 35–40 minutes, or until a skewer inserted into the centre comes out clean. Cut into wedges and serve warm from the pan.

wheat tortillas

ingredients

makes 10

250 g/9 oz plain flour,
    plus extra for dusting
½ tsp baking powder
½ tsp salt
55 g/2 oz lard, solid vegetable fat
    or butter
175 ml/6 fl oz lukewarm water
vegetable oil, for brushing

method

1 Sift the flour, baking powder and salt into a bowl and evenly rub in the lard with your fingertips. Make a well in the centre and add enough water to mix to a soft, slightly sticky, dough.

2 Turn out the dough onto a lightly floured surface and lightly knead until smooth, then wrap in oiled clingfilm and leave to rest for 30 minutes.

3 Turn out the dough and divide into 10 pieces. Roll each piece into a thin 20-cm/8-inch round.

4 Heat a flat griddle pan or heavy frying pan until very hot. Lightly brush with oil, add a tortilla and cook for a few seconds until bubbles appear on the surface, then turn and cook the other side until lightly browned.

5 Cook the remaining tortillas in the same way, keeping the cooked ones warm under a clean tea towel. Serve the tortillas warm.

sweet breads

pecan & cranberry stollen

ingredients

makes 1 loaf

400 g/14 oz strong white flour,
    plus extra for dusting
½ tsp salt
½ tsp mixed spice
55 g/2 oz butter, diced
2 tbsp caster sugar
1 sachet easy-blend dried yeast
55 g/2 oz dried cranberries
55 g/2 oz pecan nuts, chopped
1 egg, beaten
200 ml/7 fl oz lukewarm milk
vegetable oil, for brushing
140 g/5 oz marzipan
icing sugar, for sprinkling

method

1 Sift the flour, salt and mixed spice into a bowl and evenly rub in the butter. Stir in the sugar and yeast, then add the cranberries, nuts, egg and enough milk mix to a soft dough.

2 Turn out the dough onto a lightly floured surface and knead for about 10 minutes until smooth. Return to t bowl, cover and leave to rise in a warm place for abor 1 hour, or until doubled in size. Brush a large baking sheet with oil.

3 Turn out the dough onto a lightly floured surface and lightly knead, then roll out to a 23 x 18-cm/9 x 7-inch rectangle, about 1 cm/½ inch thick. Roll the marzipar into a sausage shape about 20 cm/8 inches long, the lay it down the middle of the dough rectangle and fo over the sides to enclose it.

4 Place the stollen seam side down on the prepared baking sheet, cover and leave in a warm place for about 1 hour, or until well risen. Meanwhile, preheat the oven to 190°C/375°F/Gas Mark 5.

5 Bake in the preheated oven for 30–35 minutes, or un golden brown and the base sounds hollow when tapped. Transfer to a wire rack to cool, then sprinkle with icing sugar to serve.

banana walnut bread

ingredients

makes 1 loaf

butter, for greasing
250 ml/9 fl oz walnut oil
100 g/3½ oz demerara sugar
2 eggs
3 very ripe bananas, mashed
280 g/10 oz plain flour
1 tsp bicarbonate of soda
1 tsp baking powder
½ tsp salt
3 tbsp milk
2 tbsp natural live yogurt
½ tsp vanilla extract
60 g/2¼ oz walnuts, crushed

method

1 Preheat the oven to 180°C/350°F/Gas Mark 4. Grease 450-g/1-lb loaf tin and line with baking paper.

2 In a large bowl, cream together the oil and sugar unt blended, then beat in the eggs and mashed banana

3 Combine the flour, bicarbonate of soda, baking powder and salt, then add to the banana mixture. Po in the milk, yogurt and vanilla extract and mix togeth until blended. Stir in the crushed walnuts, then pour the batter into the greased tin.

4 Bake for 50 minutes to 1 hour, or until a skewer inserted into the middle comes out clean. Cool for 10 minutes in the tin, then turn out the bread and finish cooling on a wire rack.

apple & hazelnut bread

ingredients

makes 1 loaf

butter, for greasing
350 ml/12 fl oz warm water
1 tsp caster sugar
1 sachet easy-blend dried yeast
400 g/14 oz plain white flour, plus
    extra for dusting
400 g/14 oz wholemeal
    self-raising flour
½ tsp sea salt
125 g/4½ oz toasted hazelnuts,
    chopped
50 g/1¼ oz dried apple, chopped
1 eating apple, grated

method

1 Grease a 450-g/1-lb loaf tin and line with baking paper. Put 100 ml/3½ fl oz of the warm water in a jug, stir in the sugar and yeast and leave for 15 minutes.

2 Mix the flours, salt, nuts, dried apple and fresh apple together in a large bowl. Make a well in the centre, pour in the yeast mixture and gradually work into the flour mixture. Mix in the remaining water and bring together to form a soft dough.

3 Turn out onto a floured work surface and knead briefly. Shape the dough into a rectangle and place in the prepared tin. Cover with a warm, damp cloth and set aside in a warm place for 40 minutes until the dough has risen. Meanwhile, preheat the oven to 200°C/400°F/Gas Mark 6.

4 Remove the cloth and bake the loaf in the preheated oven for 40 minutes. Carefully lift out of the tin and return the loaf to the oven, upside down, for 10–15 minutes – the loaf should sound hollow when tapped on the bottom. Remove from the oven and leave to cool on a wire rack.

citrus bread

ingredients

makes 1 loaf

450 g/1 lb strong white flour, plus extra for dusting

½ tsp salt

50 g/1¾ oz caster sugar

1 sachet easy-blend dried yeast

50 g/1¾ oz butter, diced, plus extra for greasing

5–6 tbsp orange juice

4 tbsp lemon juice

3–4 tbsp lime juice

150 ml/5 fl oz lukewarm water

1 orange

1 lemon

1 lime

2 tbsp clear honey, for glazing

method

1 Sift the flour and salt together into a large mixing bowl. Stir in the sugar and yeast.

2 Rub the butter into the mixture with your fingertips until the mixture resembles breadcrumbs. Add the orange juice, lemon juice, lime juice and water and bring together with your fingers to form a dough.

3 Turn out the dough onto a lightly floured surface and knead for 5 minutes. Place the dough in a greased bowl, cover and leave to rise in a warm place for about 1 hour, or until doubled in size. Lightly grease a baking sheet with butter.

4 Meanwhile, finely grate the rind of the orange, lemon and lime. Knead the fruit rinds into the dough. Divide the dough into 2 balls, making one slightly bigger than the other. Place the larger ball on the prepared baking sheet and set the smaller one on top.

5 Push a floured finger through the centre of the dough. Cover and leave to rise for about 40 minutes, or until springy to the touch. Meanwhile, preheat the oven to 220°C/425°F/Gas Mark 7.

6 Bake in the preheated oven for 35 minutes. Remove from the oven and transfer to a wire rack to cool. Glaze with the clear honey.

pear & lemon plait

ingredients

makes 1 loaf

vegetable oil, for brushing
500 g/1 lb 2 oz strong white flour,
    plus extra for dusting
1 tsp salt
2 tbsp caster sugar
1 sachet easy-blend dried yeast
350 ml/12 fl oz lukewarm water
2 tbsp melted butter
finely grated rind of 2 lemons
125 g/4½ oz dried pears, chopped
milk, for glazing

method

1 Brush a large baking sheet with oil. Sift the flour into a bowl, add the salt and sugar and stir in the yeast. Make a well in the centre, add the water, butter, lemon rind and pears and mix to a soft dough.

2 Turn out the dough onto a lightly floured surface and knead for about 10 minutes, or until smooth. Return to the bowl, cover and leave to rest for 5 minutes.

3 Turn out the dough onto a lightly floured surface and lightly knead, then divide into 3 pieces. Roll each piece into a 50-cm/20-inch rope. Plait the ropes loosely, pinching the ends together to hold in place.

4 Lift the plait onto the prepared baking sheet, cover and leave in a warm place for about 1 hour, or until doubled in size. Meanwhile, preheat the oven to 190°C/375°F/Gas Mark 5.

5 Brush the plait with milk and bake in the preheated oven for 30–35 minutes, or until golden brown and firm. Transfer to a wire rack to cool.

oat & apricot breakfast rolls

ingredients

makes 8

vegetable oil, for brushing
280 g/10 oz strong white flour,
    plus extra for dusting
115 g/4 oz strong wholemeal flour
115 g/4 oz porridge oats,
    plus extra for sprinkling
1 tsp salt
1 sachet easy-blend dried yeast
150 ml/5 fl oz lukewarm milk,
    plus extra for glazing
150 ml/5 fl oz lukewarm water
1 tbsp clear honey
140 g/5 oz ready-to-eat dried
    apricots, chopped

method

1 Brush a baking sheet with oil. Sift the white flour into a large bowl, add the wholemeal flour, oats and salt, then stir in the yeast and make a well in the centre. Pour the lukewarm milk and water into a jug, add the honey and stir, then add to the dry ingredients with the apricots, mixing to a soft dough.

2 Turn out the dough onto a lightly floured surface and knead for about 10 minutes until smooth, then return to the bowl, cover and leave to rest for 5 minutes.

3 Turn out the dough and divide into 8 pieces, then shape each piece into a ball and arrange on the prepared baking sheet. Cut a cross into the top of each roll with a sharp knife.

4 Cover and leave in a warm place for about 1 hour, or until doubled in size. Meanwhile, preheat the oven to 220°C/425°F/Gas Mark 7.

5 Brush the tops of the rolls with cold milk and sprinkle with oats. Bake the rolls in the preheated oven for 15–20 minutes, or until golden brown. Transfer to a wire rack to cool.

cinnamon raisin rolls

ingredients

makes 24

dough

500 g/1 lb 2 oz strong white flour,
    plus extra for dusting

1 tsp salt

3 tbsp sugar

1 tsp easy-blend dried yeast

3 tbsp vegetable suet, diced

1 egg, lightly beaten

125 ml/4 fl oz lukewarm milk

125 ml/4 fl oz lukewarm water

oil, for brushing

filling

100 g/3½ oz caster sugar

4 tbsp demerara sugar

1 tsp ground cinnamon

85 g/3 oz butter, softened,
    plus extra for greasing

55 g/2 oz raisins or sultanas

70 g/2½ oz chopped walnuts
    or pecans

method

1 Sift the flour, salt and sugar into a bowl and stir in the yeast. Stir in the suet and make a well in the centre. Beat the egg, milk and water together in a separate bowl until well blended. Add to the well and stir into the flour mixture until a soft dough forms. Turn out onto a lightly floured work surface. Knead for 5–7 minutes, or until smooth and elastic.

2 Brush a large bowl with oil, add the dough and turn to coat to prevent a crust forming. Cover and leave to rise in a warm place for 1½–2 hours, or until doubled in size. Turn out and knead lightly to deflate. Combine the sugars and cinnamon in a small bowl.

3 Generously grease 2 x 12-hole muffin tins. Roll the dough into a large rectangle slightly less than 5 mm/¼ inch thick. Cut vertically in half. Spread the butter over both dough pieces. Sprinkle the sugar mixture over the dough, then sprinkle with the fruit and nuts.

4 Starting at one long side, tightly roll each piece into a long loaf shape. Lay seam-side down and cut into 2.5-cm/1-inch slices. Arrange each slice in a muffin tin. Cover and leave to rise again in a warm place for 30–45 minutes. Meanwhile, preheat the oven to 200°C/400°F/Gas Mark 6. Bake for 15–18 minutes, or until puffed and golden. Remove to wire racks to cool.

tropical fruit bread

ingredients

makes 1 loaf

375 g/13 oz strong white flour,
plus extra for dusting

½ tsp salt

½ tsp ground ginger

25 g/1 oz bran

1 sachet easy-blend dried yeast

2 tbsp soft light brown sugar

2 tbsp butter, diced,
plus extra for greasing

250 ml/9 fl oz lukewarm water

55 g/2 oz glacé pineapple,
finely chopped

2 tbsp finely chopped dried mango

70 g/2½ oz grated coconut,
toasted, plus extra for
sprinkling

1 egg, lightly beaten

method

1 Grease a baking sheet. Sift the flour, salt and ginger together into a large warmed bowl. Stir in the bran, yeast and sugar. Rub in the butter with your fingertips until the mixture resembles breadcrumbs. Add the water and mix to form a dough.

2 Turn out the dough onto a lightly floured work surface and knead for 5–10 minutes, or until smooth and elastic. Put the dough in a greased bowl, cover with clingfilm and leave to rise in a warm place for 30 minutes, or until doubled in size.

3 Turn out the dough again and knead in the pineapple, mango and coconut. Shape into a round and transfer to the prepared baking sheet. Score the top with the back of a knife. Cover with clingfilm and leave in a warm place for 30 minutes. Preheat the oven to 220°C/425°F/Gas Mark 7.

4 Brush the loaf with the beaten egg and sprinkle with coconut. Bake in the preheated oven for 30 minutes, until golden brown. Transfer to a wire rack to cool.

malted fruit loaf

ingredients

makes 1 loaf

350 g/12 oz plain flour,
    plus extra for dusting
1 tsp salt
1 tsp easy-blend dried yeast
140 g/5 oz sultanas
200 ml/7 fl oz lukewarm water
2 tsp vegetable oil,
    plus extra for brushing
2 tbsp malt extract
1½ tbsp treacle

method

1 Sift the flour and salt together into a bowl and stir in
the yeast and sultanas. Make a well in the centre and
pour in the water, vegetable oil, malt extract and
treacle. Stir well with a wooden spoon until the doug
begins to come together, then knead with your hand
until it leaves the side of the bowl. Turn out onto a
lightly floured surface and knead well for about
10 minutes, or until smooth and elastic.

2 Brush a bowl with oil. Shape the dough into a ball, pu
in the bowl and cover. Leave to rise in a warm place fo
1–2 hours, or until the dough has doubled in volume.

3 Brush a 900-g/2-lb loaf tin with oil. Turn out the doug
onto a lightly floured surface and knead for 1 minute
With lightly floured hands, flatten the dough into a
rectangle the same width as the tin. Fold it into 3 and
place in the prepared tin, seam side down. Cover and
leave to rise in a warm place for 30–40 minutes, or un
the dough has reached the top of the tin.

4 Meanwhile, preheat the oven to 230°C/450°F/Gas Mark
Bake the loaf for 30–40 minutes, or until it has shrunk
from the sides of the tin, the crust is golden brown a
it sounds hollow when tapped on the base with you
knuckles. Turn out onto a wire rack to cool.

spiced pumpkin bread

ingredients
makes 1 loaf

vegetable oil, for brushing
450 g/1 lb pumpkin flesh
115 g/4 oz butter, softened,
    plus extra for greasing
100 g/3½ oz caster sugar
2 eggs, lightly beaten
225 g/8 oz plain flour
1½ tsp baking powder
½ tsp salt
1 tsp ground mixed spice
2 tbsp pumpkin seeds

method

1 Preheat the oven to 200°C/400°F/Gas Mark 6. Brush a 900-g/2-lb loaf tin with oil.

2 Chop the pumpkin into large pieces and wrap in buttered foil. Cook in the oven for 30–40 minutes until they are tender. Reduce the oven temperature to 160°C/325°F/Gas Mark 3. Let the pumpkin cool completely before mashing well to make a thick paste.

3 In a bowl, cream the butter and sugar together until light and fluffy. Add the beaten eggs, a little at a time. Stir in the pumpkin paste then sift in the flour, baking powder, salt and mixed spice.

4 Fold the pumpkin seeds gently through the mixture in a figure-of-eight movement. Spoon the mixture into the prepared loaf tin. Bake in the oven for about 1¼–1½ hours, or until a skewer inserted into the centre of the loaf comes out clean. Transfer to a wire rack to cool.

barm brack

ingredients

makes 1 loaf

650 g/1lb 7 oz strong white flour,
    plus extra for dusting

1 tsp mixed spice

1 tsp salt

2 tsp easy-blend dried yeast

1 tbsp sugar

300 ml/10 fl oz lukewarm milk

150 ml/5 fl oz lukewarm water

vegetable oil, for brushing

50 g/1¾oz lightly salted butter,
    softened, plus extra to serve

250 g/9 oz mixed dried fruit, such
    as sultanas, currants and raisins

milk, for glazing

method

1 Sift the flour, mixed spice and salt into a warm bowl. S
    in the yeast and sugar. Make a well in the centre and
    pour in the milk and water. Mix well to make a sticky
    dough. Turn the dough out onto a lightly floured wor
    surface and knead until no longer sticky. Put the doug
    in an oiled bowl, cover with clingfilm and leave to rise
    in a warm place for 1 hour, or until doubled in size.

2 Turn the dough out onto a floured work surface and
    knead lightly for 1 minute. Add the butter and dried
    fruit to the dough and work them in until completely
    incorporated. Return the dough to the bowl, cover an
    leave to rise for 30 minutes.

3 Brush a 23-cm/9-inch round cake tin with oil. Pat the
    dough into a neat circle and fit in the tin. Cover and
    leave in a warm place until the dough has risen to
    the top of the tin. Meanwhile, preheat the oven to
    200°C/400°F/Gas Mark 6.

4 Brush the top of the loaf lightly with milk and bake in t
    preheated oven for 15 minutes. Cover with foil, reduce
    the oven temperature to 180°C/350°F/Gas Mark 4, and
    bake for an additional 45 minutes, or until golden brow
    and it sounds hollow when tapped on the base. Transf
    to a wire rack to cool.

bran & yogurt bread

ingredients

makes 1 small loaf

200 g/7 oz strong white flour, plus
    extra for dusting
150 g/5½ oz strong
    wholemeal flour
1 tsp salt
¾ tsp easy-blend dried yeast
25 g/1 oz wheat bran
150 ml/5 fl oz lukewarm water
125 ml/4 fl oz natural yogurt
1 tbsp vegetable oil,
    plus extra for brushing
1 tbsp treacle or golden syrup

method

1 Sift both types of flour and the salt together into a bowl and tip in the bran from the sieve. Stir in the yeast and wheat bran. Make a well in the centre and pour in the water, yogurt, oil and treacle. Stir well with a wooden spoon until the dough begins to come together, then knead with your hands until it leaves the side of the bowl. Turn out onto a lightly floured surface and knead well for about 10 minutes, or until smooth and elastic.

2 Brush a bowl with oil. Shape the dough into a ball, put it in the bowl and cover. Leave to rise in a warm place for 1–2 hours, or until the dough has doubled in size.

3 Brush a baking sheet with oil. Turn out the dough onto a lightly floured surface, knock back with your fist and knead for 1 minute. With lightly floured hands, shape the dough into a ball and flatten slightly. Put the loaf onto the prepared baking sheet, cover and leave to rise in a warm place for 30 minutes.

4 Preheat the oven to 220°C/425°F/Gas Mark 7. Slash the top of the loaf and bake for 30 minutes, or until golden brown and it sounds hollow when tapped on the base with your knuckles. Transfer to a wire rack to cool.

muesli bread

ingredients

makes 1 loaf

300 g/10½ oz strong white flour,
    plus extra for dusting
85 g/3 oz strong wholemeal flour
1½ tsp salt
150 g/5½ oz unsweetened muesli
3 tbsp skimmed milk powder
1 sachet easy-blend dried yeast
250 ml/9 fl oz lukewarm water
2 tbsp vegetable oil, plus extra
    for brushing
1 tbsp clear honey
70 g/2½ oz ready-to-eat dried
    apricots, chopped

method

1 Sift the flours and salt together into a bowl and tip in
the bran from the sieve. Stir in the muesli, milk powder
and yeast. Make a well in the centre and pour in the
water, oil and honey. Stir well until the dough begins to
come together, then knead until it leaves the side of
the bowl. Turn out onto a lightly floured surface and
knead well for 5 minutes. Knead in the apricots and
continue to knead for a further 5 minutes, or until the
dough is smooth and elastic.

2 Brush a bowl with oil. Shape the dough into a ball, put
it in the bowl and cover. Leave to rise in a warm place
for 1 hour, or until doubled in size.

3 Brush a baking sheet with oil. Turn out the dough onto
a lightly floured surface and knead briefly for 1 minute.
With lightly floured hands, shape the dough into a
round and place on the prepared baking sheet. Cut a
cross in the top of the loaf. Cover and leave to rise in a
warm place for 30–40 minutes. Meanwhile, preheat the
oven to 200°C/400°F/Gas Mark 6.

4 Bake the loaf for 30–35 minutes, or until firm and
golden brown. Transfer to a wire rack to cool.

lavender & honey spirals

ingredients

makes 9

450 g/1 lb strong white flour, plus
    extra for dusting
1 tsp salt
1 sachet easy-blend dried yeast
300 ml/10 fl oz lukewarm milk,
    plus extra for glazing
3 tbsp lavender honey
50 g/1¾oz melted butter, plus
    extra for greasing
1 tbsp dried lavender flowers
1 tbsp demerara sugar

method

1 Grease a 23-cm/9-inch round spring-form cake tin with butter. Place the flour and salt in a bowl and stir in the yeast. Make a well in the centre and add the milk, 2 tablespoons of the honey and 2 tablespoons of the butter, mixing to a soft dough.

2 Turn out the dough onto a lightly floured surface and knead for about 10 minutes until smooth, then return to the bowl, cover and leave to rest for 5 minutes.

3 Turn out the dough onto a lightly floured surface and lightly knead again. Roll out to a 25 x 30-cm/10 x 12-inch rectangle. Brush with the remaining butter and sprinkle with the lavender flowers and sugar.

4 Firmly roll up the dough from one long edge, then cut into 9 equal slices and arrange in the prepared tin, cut side up.

5 Cover and leave in a warm place for about 1 hour, or until the dough has doubled in size. Meanwhile, preheat the oven to 190°C/375°F/Gas Mark 5.

6 Brush the spirals with milk and bake in the preheated oven for 30–35 minutes, or until golden brown. Warm the remaining honey and brush over the surface of the spirals, then remove from the tin and transfer to a wire rack to cool. Pull the spirals apart to serve.

chocolate bread

ingredients

makes 1 loaf

450 g/1 lb strong white flour, plus
    extra for dusting
1 tsp salt
25 g/1 oz cocoa powder
1 sachet easy-blend dried yeast
2 tbsp soft light brown sugar
1 tbsp oil, plus extra for brushing
300 ml/10 fl oz lukewarm water
butter, for greasing

method

1 Sift the flour, salt and cocoa powder together into a
large bowl. Stir in the yeast and sugar. Make a well in
the centre. Add the oil and water to the well and mix
form a dough.

2 Turn out the dough onto a lightly floured work surfac
and knead for 5–10 minutes, or until smooth and
elastic. Put the dough in an oiled bowl, cover and leav
to rise in a warm place for 1 hour, or until doubled in
size. Lightly grease a 900-g/2-lb loaf tin.

3 Turn out the dough again and knead lightly for
1 minute. Shape into a loaf. Transfer the dough to the
prepared tin, cover and leave in a warm place for
30 minutes. Meanwhile, preheat the oven to
200°C/400°F/Gas Mark 6.

4 Bake the loaf in the preheated oven for 25–30 minute
or until it sounds hollow when tapped on the base.
Transfer the loaf to a wire rack to cool.

italian chocolate chip bread

ingredients

makes 1 loaf

vegetable oil, for brushing
225 g/8 oz plain flour,
    plus extra for dusting
1 tbsp cocoa powder
pinch of salt
15 g/½ oz butter, plus ½ tsp
    melted butter for brushing
1 tbsp caster sugar
1 sachet easy-blend dried yeast
150 ml/5 fl oz lukewarm water
55 g/2 oz plain chocolate chips

method

1 Brush a baking sheet with oil. Sift the flour, cocoa powder and salt together into a bowl. Add the butter and cut it into the dry ingredients, then stir in the sugar and yeast.

2 Gradually add the water, stirring well with a wooden spoon until the dough begins to come together, then knead with your hands until it leaves the side of the bowl. Turn out onto a lightly floured surface and knead for about 10 minutes, or until smooth and elastic.

3 Knead the chocolate chips into the dough, then form into a round loaf. Put the loaf onto the prepared baking sheet and cover. Leave to rise in a warm place for 1–1½ hours, or until the dough has doubled in size. Preheat the oven to 220°C/425°F/Gas Mark 7.

4 Bake the loaf in the preheated oven for 10 minutes, then reduce the oven temperature to 190°C/375°F/Gas Mark 5 and bake for a further 15 minutes. Transfer the loaf to a wire rack and brush the top with the melted butter. Cover with a tea towel and leave to cool.

gluten-free recipes

buckwheat soda bread

ingredients
makes 1 loaf

140 g/5 oz buckwheat flour,
   plus extra for sprinkling
100 g/3½ oz rice flour
1 tsp salt
1 tsp xanthan gum
2 tsp gluten-free baking powder
300 ml/10 fl oz milk,
   plus extra for glazing
1 tsp white wine vinegar
1 tbsp olive oil

method

1 Preheat the oven to 200°C/400°F/Gas Mark 6. Sift the buckwheat flour, rice flour, salt, xanthan gum and baking powder together into a bowl and make a well the centre.

2 Mix together the milk, vinegar and oil and stir into the dry ingredients to make a very soft dough.

3 Sprinkle a little flour over a baking sheet. Shape the dough into a smooth 20-cm/8-inch round and place on the baking sheet. Lightly press to flatten, then use sharp knife to cut a deep cross into the loaf.

4 Brush with milk to glaze and bake in the preheated oven for 25–30 minutes, or until risen, firm and golde brown. Transfer to a wire rack to cool.

gluten-free flatbreads

ingredients

makes 4

200 g/7 oz buckwheat flour,
    plus extra for dusting
100 g/3½ oz rice flour
1 tsp salt
1 tsp gluten-free baking powder
½ tsp ground cumin
2 tbsp chopped fresh coriander
200 ml/7 fl oz water
2 tbsp olive oil

method

1 Sift the buckwheat flour, rice flour, salt, baking powder and cumin together into a large bowl and make a well in the centre.

2 Add the coriander, water and oil and stir into the dry ingredients to make a soft dough.

3 Divide the dough into 4 pieces and shape each piece into a smooth ball. Roll out each ball on a lightly floured surface to a 20-cm/8-inch round.

4 Preheat a griddle pan or barbecue to very hot. Add the flatbreads and cook for about 1 minute on each side, until firm and golden brown. Serve warm.

soft corn tortillas

ingredients

makes 12

225 g/8 oz masa harina (ground
cornmeal treated with lime)

¼ tsp salt

300 ml/10 fl oz lukewarm water

method

1 Put the masa harina and salt into a bowl and make a well in the centre. Stir in just enough of the water to mix to a moist, firm dough. Cover and leave to stand fo 15 minutes.

2 Divide the dough into 12 pieces, roll each piece into a smooth ball, then place between 2 sheets of clingfilm and roll with a rolling pin (or use a tortilla press) to a thin 20-cm/8-inch round.

3 Heat a flat griddle pan or frying pan until very hot, place a tortilla on it, cook for about 20 seconds, then flip over. Cook for a further 20 seconds, then turn once more and cook until it puffs slightly.

4 Remove from the pan, cover with a clean tea towel and keep warm while cooking the remaining tortillas. Serve warm.

quick tomato focaccia

ingredients

makes 1 loaf

3 tbsp olive oil, plus extra for
    brushing
200 g/7 oz buckwheat flour
200 g/7 oz potato flour
200 g/7 oz rice flour
2 tsp xanthan gum
1 sachet gluten-free,
    easy-blend dried yeast
1½ tsp salt
½ tsp black onion seeds
40 g/1½ oz sun-dried tomatoes,
    soaked, drained and chopped
600 ml/1 pint tepid water
1 small egg, beaten
2 garlic cloves, cut into slivers
few sprigs fresh oregano

method

1 Brush a 33 x 23-cm/13 x 9-inch baking sheet with oil.
   Mix the flours, xanthan gum, yeast, salt and onion seeds
   in a bowl and stir in the tomatoes.

2 Make a well in the centre and stir in the water, egg and
   1 tablespoon of oil to make a very soft dough. Beat the
   dough hard using a wooden spoon for 4–5 minutes,
   then spoon into the tin, spreading evenly with a
   palette knife.

3 Cover with oiled cling film and leave in a warm place
   for about 1 hour, or until doubled in size. Preheat the
   oven to 220°C/425°F/Gas Mark 7.

4 Press pieces of garlic and oregano into the dough at
   intervals. Drizzle with the remaining oil, then bake in
   the oven for 25–30 minutes, or until firm and golden
   brown. Turn out and cool on a wire rack.

red pepper cornbread

ingredients

makes 1 loaf

1 large red pepper, deseeded
    and sliced
175 g/6 oz fine cornmeal
    or polenta
115 g/4 oz gluten-free plain flour
1 tbsp gluten-free baking powder
1 tsp salt
2 tsp demerara sugar
250 ml/9 fl oz milk
2 eggs, lightly beaten
3 tbsp olive oil,
    plus extra for brushing

method

1 Preheat the oven to 200°C/400°F/Gas Mark 6. Arrange the red pepper slices on a baking tray and roast in the preheated oven for 35 minutes until tender and the skin begins to blister. Set aside to cool slightly, then peel away the skin.

2 Meanwhile, mix the cornmeal, flour, baking powder, salt and sugar together in a large mixing bowl. Beat the milk, eggs and oil together in a separate bowl or jug and gradually add to the cornmeal mixture. Beat with a wooden spoon to make a thick, smooth, batter-like consistency.

3 Brush a 450-g/1-lb loaf tin with oil. Finely chop the red pepper and fold into the cornmeal mixture, then spoon into the prepared tin. Bake in the preheated oven for 30 minutes until lightly golden. Leave in the tin for 10 minutes, then run a knife around the edge of the tin and turn the loaf out onto a wire rack to cool.

courgette & polenta bread squares

ingredients

makes 9

vegetable oil, for brushing
150 g/5½ oz polenta
100 g/3½ oz soya flour
1 tbsp gluten-free baking powder
1 tsp salt
½ tsp pepper
225 g/8 oz courgettes, grated
1 large egg, beaten
300 ml/10 fl oz unsweetened
   soya milk
3 tbsp olive oil

method

1 Preheat the oven to 190°C/375°F/Gas Mark 5. Brush a 19-cm/7½-inch shallow, square cake tin with oil.

2 Put the polenta, flour, baking powder, salt and pepper into a bowl. Stir in the courgettes.

3 Beat together the egg, milk and oil and stir into the dry ingredients, mixing evenly to a soft batter.

4 Spoon the mixture into the prepared tin and smooth level with a palette knife.

5 Bake in the preheated oven for 30–35 minutes, or until firm and golden brown. Leave to cool for 10 minutes in the tin, then cut into squares to serve.

gruyère & mustard slice

ingredients

makes 1 loaf

200 g/7 oz buckwheat flour
200 g/7 oz potato flour
100 g/3½ oz rice flour
1½ tsp salt
2 tsp xanthan gum
1 sachet gluten-free,
  easy-blend dried yeast
300 ml/10 fl oz lukewarm water
1 small egg, beaten
1 tbsp olive oil,
  plus extra for brushing
2 tbsp gluten-free
  wholegrain mustard
115 g/4 oz Gruyère cheese, grated

method

1 Brush a 33 x 23-cm/13 x 9-inch baking sheet with oil. Sift the buckwheat flour, potato flour, rice flour, salt and xanthan gum together into a bowl, then stir in the yeast.

2 Make a well in the centre and stir in the water, egg and oil to make a very soft dough. Beat with a wooden spoon for about 1 minute, or until smooth. Divide the dough into 2 pieces.

3 Brush a work surface with oil and roll out 1 piece of the dough. Use the rolling pin to lift it into the prepared tin, pressing out with your knuckles. Spread the dough with the mustard and sprinkle with about two thirds of the cheese.

4 Roll out the remaining dough to cover the first piece, pressing with your fingers to make indentations in the dough. Cover and leave in a warm place for about 1 hour, or until doubled in size. Meanwhile, preheat the oven to 220°C/425°F/Gas Mark 7.

5 Sprinkle the remaining cheese over the dough and bake in the preheated oven for 25–30 minutes, or until firm and golden brown. Transfer to a wire rack to cool.

parmesan & garlic rolls

ingredients

makes 12

2 tbsp olive oil, plus extra
    for brushing
3 garlic cloves, crushed
400 g/14 oz gluten-free,
    wheat-free, strong white flour,
    plus extra for dusting
1½ tsp salt
1 sachet gluten-free,
    easy-blend dried yeast
55 g/2 oz finely grated
    Parmesan cheese
300 ml/10 fl oz lukewarm water
milk, for glazing

method

1 Brush a baking sheet with oil. Heat the 2 tablespoons of oil in a saucepan, add the garlic and gently stir-fry for about 1 minute, without browning. Remove from the heat and leave to cool slightly.

2 Sift together the flour and salt into a bowl, then stir in the yeast and three-quarters of the cheese. Make a well in the centre and add the water and garlic oil, stirring to make a soft dough.

3 Turn out the dough onto a lightly floured surface and lightly knead until smooth. Divide into 12 pieces and shape each piece into a smooth round.

4 Place the rounds on the prepared baking sheet and cut a deep cross into the top of each one with a sharp knife. Cover and leave in a warm place for about 1 hour or until doubled in size. Meanwhile, preheat the oven to 200°C/400°F/Gas Mark 6.

5 Brush the tops of the rolls with milk and sprinkle with the remaining cheese. Bake in the preheated oven for 12–15 minutes, or until firm and golden brown. Transfer to a wire rack to cool.

quinoa & chive rolls

ingredients

makes 8

200 g/7 oz buckwheat flour
150 g/5½ oz potato flour
2 tsp xanthan gum
1½ tsp salt
1 sachet gluten-free,
    easy-blend dried yeast
100 g/3½ oz quinoa
3 tbsp snipped chives
350 ml/12 fl oz lukewarm water
1 small egg, beaten
1 tbsp olive oil,
    plus extra for brushing
milk, for glazing

method

1 Brush a large baking sheet with oil. Sift the buckwheat flour, potato flour, xanthan gum and salt together into bowl, then stir in the yeast, quinoa and chives.

2 Make a well in the centre and stir in the water, egg and oil to make a soft dough. Very lightly knead the dough until smooth.

3 Divide the dough into 8 pieces and shape each piece into a smooth ball. Arrange on the prepared baking sheet, cover and leave in a warm place for about 1 hour, or until doubled in size. Meanwhile, preheat the oven to 200°C/400°F/Gas Mark 6.

4 Brush the rolls with milk to glaze. Bake in the preheated oven for 20–25 minutes, or until firm and golden brown. Transfer to a wire rack to cool.

chicken & basil pizza

ingredients

serves 2–4

vegetable oil, for brushing
350 g/12 oz gluten-free,
    wheat-free, white bread flour
1 tsp salt
1 sachet gluten-free,
    easy-blend dried yeast
250 ml/9 fl oz lukewarm water
2 tbsp olive oil

topping

200 g/7 oz chunky passata
1 red onion, thinly sliced
3 tbsp chopped fresh basil,
    plus extra to garnish
200 g/7 oz cooked chicken, diced
100 g/3½ oz mozzarella cheese,
    diced
salt and pepper

method

1 Brush a large baking sheet with oil. Sift the flour and salt into a bowl and stir in the yeast. Make a well in the centre, add the water with 1 tablespoon of the oil and lightly mix to form a soft dough.

2 Lightly knead the dough to a smooth ball, then roll out to a 35-cm/14-inch round on the prepared baking sheet, pinching the edges slightly to make a raised edge. Cover and leave in a warm place for 1–1½ hours or until well risen and springy to the touch.

3 Preheat the oven to 200°C/400°F/Gas Mark 6. Spread the passata over the dough to within 1 cm/½ inch of the edge. Scatter over the onion, basil and chicken, then top with the cheese. Sprinkle with salt and pepper to taste, then sprinkle with the remaining oil.

4 Bake in the preheated oven for 25–30 minutes, or until firm and golden. Sprinkle with basil and serve hot.

shallot & bacon loaf

ingredients

makes 1 small loaf

vegetable oil, for brushing
1 tbsp olive oil
2 shallots, thinly sliced
85 g/3 oz streaky bacon or
    pancetta, finely chopped
250 g/9 oz gluten-free,
    wheat-free, brown bread flour
½ tsp salt
1 tsp gluten-free, easy-blend
    dried yeast
1 tbsp maple syrup
225 ml/8 fl oz lukewarm water

method

1 Brush a 450-g/1-lb loaf tin with oil and base-line with non-stick baking paper. Heat the oil in a frying pan, then add the shallots and bacon and fry for about 5 minutes, stirring occasionally, or until soft and golden. Remove from the heat and leave to cool slightly.

2 Mix the flour, salt and yeast in a bowl and make a well in the centre.

3 Mix together the maple syrup and water and stir into the dry ingredients with the shallots and bacon, lightly mixing to form a very soft, sticky dough.

4 Spoon the dough into the prepared tin and spread evenly. Cover with oiled clingfilm and leave in a warm place for about 1 hour, or until the dough has risen and is spongy to the touch. Meanwhile, preheat the oven to 200°C/400°F/Gas Mark 6.

5 Bake in the preheated oven for 30–35 minutes, or until golden brown and firm. Serve warm.

orange & mint rolls

ingredients

makes 12

400 g/14 oz gluten-free,
    wheat-free, strong white flour,
    plus extra for dusting
1 tsp salt
85 g/3 oz light muscovado sugar
1 sachet gluten-free, easy-blend
    dried yeast
½ tsp dried mint
finely grated rind of 1 orange
100 ml/3½ fl oz orange juice,
    plus extra for glazing
1 tbsp sunflower oil,
    plus extra for glazing
300 ml/10 fl oz lukewarm water

method

1 Brush a large baking sheet with oil. Sift the flour and
  salt together into a bowl, then stir in the sugar, yeast
  and mint. Make a well in the centre and add the orange
  rind, orange juice, oil and enough water to mix to a
  very soft dough.

2 Turn out the dough onto a lightly floured surface and
  very lightly knead until smooth. Divide into 12 pieces,
  shape each piece into a round and place on the
  prepared baking sheet.

3 Lightly press the rounds to flatten, then cut 3 slashes
  across the top of each roll with a sharp knife. Cover
  with oiled clingfilm and leave in a warm place for
  about 1 hour, or until well risen. Meanwhile, preheat
  the oven to 200°C/400°F/Gas Mark 6.

4 Brush the rolls with orange juice to glaze. Bake in the
  preheated oven for 12–15 minutes, or until golden
  brown and firm. Transfer to a wire rack to cool.

cinnamon & cranberry bread

ingredients

makes 1 loaf

oil, for brushing
400 g/14 oz gluten-free,
    wheat-free, strong white flour,
    plus extra for dusting
85 g/3 oz light muscovado sugar
1½ tsp ground cinnamon
1 sachet gluten-free,
    easy-blend dried yeast
55 g/2 oz dried cranberries
250 ml/9 fl oz lukewarm
    cranberry juice
1 egg, beaten
2 tbsp melted butter

method

1 Brush a baking sheet with oil. Sift the flour, sugar and cinnamon together into a bowl and stir in the yeast and cranberries.

2 Make a well in the centre and stir in the cranberry juice, egg and butter to make a very soft dough. Beat with a wooden spoon for 2 minutes.

3 Turn out onto a lightly floured surface and shape the dough into a 35-cm/12-inch long roll. Place on the prepared baking sheet, cover with oiled clingfilm and leave in a warm place for about 1 hour, or until doubled in size. Meanwhile, preheat the oven to 200°C/400°F/Gas Mark 6.

4 Bake the loaf in the preheated oven for 35–40 minutes, or until firm and golden brown. Transfer to a wire rack to cool.

gluten-free hot cross buns

ingredients

makes 12

vegetable oil, for brushing
450 g/1 lb gluten-free,
    wheat-free, white bread flour
1 tsp salt
2 tsp mixed spice
1 sachet gluten-free,
    easy-blend dried yeast
2 large eggs, beaten
2 tbsp melted butter
4 tbsp clear honey
3–4 tsp lemon juice
200 g/7 oz mixed dried fruit
325 ml/11 fl oz lukewarm milk
85 g/3 oz icing sugar

method

1 Brush a large baking sheet with oil. Sift the flour, salt and spice into a bowl and stir in the yeast.

2 Make a well in the centre and add the eggs, butter, honey, 1 teaspoon of the lemon juice and the dried fruit, with enough milk to mix to a soft, sticky dough.

3 Place 12 large, smooth spoonfuls of the dough on the prepared baking sheet (a large ice cream scoop is useful). Cover with oiled clingfilm and leave in a warm place for 1–1½ hours, or until well risen and puffy. Meanwhile, preheat the oven to 220°C/425°F/Gas Mark 7.

4 Bake in the preheated oven for 15–20 minutes, or until firm and golden brown. Transfer to a wire rack to cool.

5 Mix the icing sugar with enough of the remaining lemon juice to make a thick paste, then spoon or pipe the paste on top of each bun to make a cross.

sweet almond & apricot loaf

ingredients

makes 1 loaf

400 g/14 oz gluten-free,
    wheat-free, strong white flour
115 g/4 oz caster sugar
1 sachet gluten-free,
    easy-blend dried yeast
70 g/2½ oz ground almonds
115 g/4 oz ready-to-eat dried
    apricots, chopped
2 eggs, beaten
300 ml/10 fl oz lukewarm milk
1 tbsp sunflower oil,
    plus extra for brushing
1 tbsp flaked almonds

method

1 Brush a 900-g/2-lb loaf tin with oil and base-line with non-stick baking paper. Sift the flour, sugar and yeast together into a bowl and stir in the ground almonds and apricots.

2 Make a well in the centre and stir in the eggs, milk and oil to make a soft, sticky dough. Beat with a wooden spoon for 2 minutes. Spoon the dough into the prepared tin, spreading evenly with a palette knife.

3 Cover with oiled clingfilm and leave in a warm place for about 1 hour, or until well risen and springy to the touch. Meanwhile, preheat the oven to 200°C/400°F/Gas Mark 6.

4 Sprinkle with flaked almonds, then bake the loaf in the preheated oven for 30–35 minutes, or until firm and golden brown. Turn out and transfer to a wire rack to cool.

banana & brazil nut loaf

ingredients

makes 1 loaf

55 g/2 oz soya flour
55 g/2 oz gluten-free cornflour
70 g/2½ oz tapioca flour
2 tsp gluten-free baking powder
½ tsp xanthan gum
2 tsp mixed spice
85 g/3 oz light muscovado sugar
2 eggs, beaten
1 tsp vanilla extract
4 tbsp sunflower oil,
    plus extra for brushing
3 very ripe bananas, mashed
100 g/3½ oz brazil nuts, chopped

method

1 Brush a 900-g/2-lb loaf tin with oil and line with baking paper. Preheat the oven to 180°C/350°F/Gas Mark 4.

2 Sift the soya flour, cornflour, tapioca flour, baking powder, xanthan gum and mixed spice together into bowl and add the sugar, eggs, vanilla extract, oil and bananas. Beat well with a wooden spoon or an electric whisk until a thick batter forms.

3 Fold in the chopped nuts and spoon the mixture into the prepared tin. Bake the loaf in the preheated oven for 45–50 minutes, or until golden brown and firm.

4 Leave to cool in the tin for 10 minutes, then turn out and transfer to a wire rack to cool completely.

208 *index*

index